WITHOUT CONSENT

The Ethics of Disclosing Personal
Information in Public Archives

Heather MacNeil

The Society of American Archivists

and

The Scarecrow Press, Inc.
Metuchen, N.J., and London

1992

This book is based on the author's Master of Archival Studies thesis, "In Search of the Common Good: The Ethics of Disclosing Personal Information Held in Public Archives," University of British Columbia, 1987.

British Library Cataloguing-in-Publication data available

Library of Congress Cataloging-in-Publication Data

MacNeil, Heather.
  Without consent : the ethics of disclosing personal information in public archives / Heather MacNeil.
    p. cm.
  Includes bibliographical references and index.
  ISBN 0-8108-2581-3 (acid-free paper)
  1. Archives—Access control. 2. Privacy, Right of. I. Title.
CD986.5.M33 1992
350.71'46—dc20   92-16754

Copyright © 1992 by Heather MacNeil
Manufactured in the United States of America
Printed on acid-free paper

Contents

Introduction	1
Defining Moral and Legal Zones of Privacy	9
Living for the Record *The Individual, the State, and the Emergence of a Right to Information Privacy*	35
In Search of the Public Good *Balancing the Right to Privacy and the Right to Know*	61
Documenting the Lives of the Laboring and Unlettered *The Use of Archival Sources for Socio-Historical Research*	103
The Administration of Access to Personal Information Held in Public Archives *Common Problems and Practices*	127
Research Uses of Personal Information *Some Ethical Considerations*	155
Administering Access to Personal Information in Government Archives *Some Modest Proposals*	181
Selected Bibliography	205
Index	219

Acknowledgments

During the years in which I was researching the thesis that eventually evolved into this book, I was a student in the Master of Archival Studies Program at the University of British Columbia. I would like to acknowledge a permanent debt to Terry Eastwood, director of the program, and Hugh Taylor, adjunct professor, both of whom have shaped my sensibility as an archivist in incalculable ways.

Many people contributed to this book in specific ways. I would like to thank Anne Piternick, who submitted the abstract of the thesis on which this book is based to Scarecrow Press.

For their unfailing courtesy and helpfulness in responding to my many requests for information I am indebted to Judy Jean, Yves Marcoux, and Diane Ménard of the Canadian Centre for Information and Documentation on Archives; and to Rhoda Zaitlin of the library of the Canadian Information and Privacy Commissioner's Office.

I am grateful to Roy Maddocks for several conversations that clarified my understanding of the administration of access to archival records under Canadian privacy legislation. Any misunderstandings that remain are my own.

I would like to give particular thanks to Kent Haworth who remained an unreservedly supportive employer and friend throughout the writing of this book and the thesis that preceded it.

Finally, I owe a special debt of gratitude to Debra Barr who commented thoughtfully on numerous drafts of the manuscript and consistently offered valuable advice and encouragement when I most needed it.

Introduction

In 1890, Samuel Warren and Louis Brandeis published "The Right to Privacy [the implicit made explicit]" in the *Harvard Law Review*.[1] In their article, which was to become a watershed in the development of American common law, the authors eloquently argued the case for the legal protection of a right to privacy. The explicit recognition of such a right was intended to protect individuals against the unjustifiable exposure of their private affairs without their consent, an exposure which, Warren and Brandeis averred, "subjected [an individual] to mental pain and distress, far greater than could be inflicted by mere bodily agony."[2] Jurists, legislators, and civil libertarians have been trying to define the moral and legal contours of the right to privacy ever since.

Our moral interest in privacy, and the grounds on which we claim a legal right to it, derives from a respect for individual autonomy, expressed as the individuals' freedom from the scrutiny and judgment of others in certain areas of their lives. The association of privacy with individual moral autonomy developed gradually in western culture. In ancient feeling, the privative aspect of privacy was emphasized; the word *private* meant literally a state of being deprived of something and suggested a withdrawing from public life that was generally viewed in a negative light. Aristotle, for example, insisted that an individual who lived only a private life could not be fully human. But according to Raymond Williams, who has traced the etymology of the word, around the fifteenth century, *private* acquired a slightly different meaning that manifested itself in "a conventional opposition to public, as in private house, private education, . . . private club, private property. In virtually all these uses the primary sense was one of privilege; the limited access or participation was seen not as deprivation but as advantage."[3]

Equally important was the gradual replacement of the senses of "withdrawal" and "seclusion," associated with privacy, by those of "independence" and "intimacy." Beginning around the sixteenth century and continuing into the seventeenth and eighteenth centuries, Williams suggests, "seclusion, in the sense of a quiet life [increasingly] was valued as privacy, develop[ing] beyond the sense of solitude to the senses of decent and dignified withdrawal . . . and beyond these to the generalized values of private life."[4] This last development was closely connected to the emergence of modern individualism in the eighteenth century, during which time, "Hobbes, then Locke, and eventually Rousseau gave credence to the individual and the individual's role in the larger community."[5]

The modern notion of privacy as inhabiting a psychological as well as a geographical sphere, was born, at least partly, in rebellion against the increasingly oppressive intrusion of society and, especially, the state, into the lives of its citizens. Today, aided by the enormous growth of technology, the societal imperatives that first created the modern demand for privacy threaten to erode the more recently established boundary between the public and private spheres. Some historians have argued that we experience greater privacy than did earlier generations.[6] The weakening of community bonds and moral norms, the anonymity of urban life, and the increased cultural emphasis on individual aspiration and achievement are cited frequently as factors that have enhanced individual privacy significantly.[7] But, as the philosopher Arthur Schafer argues, the social impact of these factors has not been so profound as that caused by such countervailing historical trends as the higher population density of urban environments; business factors, such as the widespread use of credit with the resultant need for credit ratings; and, perhaps most significantly, the technological breakthroughs in computerization and monitoring, which permit extensive government and business surveillance of private affairs and communication.[8]

Contemporary concerns over losses of privacy relate for the most part to the amount of information known about an individual, and have emerged in response to situations created by information-gathering practices ignored in traditional interpretations of invasion of privacy. The threat to the individual's privacy in this area is embodied most strikingly in the benign surveillance power of large information-gathering organizations in society. Advances in computer technologies have resulted in the enormous expansion of the capacity of government data banks, for example, to organize, store, and retrieve personal information on citizens. Civil libertarians maintain that, even if nothing intrinsically private or improperly derogatory is stored in a data bank, the possibility exists that the vast quantities of ostensibly innocuous information on citizens, combined with the technological capacity to link information from a variety of sources, will result in a less spontaneous and, ultimately, less free society. Over the last twenty years, growing citizen concern over potential and actual abuses of personal information held in large recordkeeping systems has forced most western countries to develop data protection laws which attempt to define categories of private life as these relate to recordkeeping practices, and defend them against arbitrary invasions. Since government recordkeeping practices are widely perceived as carrying the greatest potential threat to information privacy, such laws have been directed primarily at government agencies.

The right to privacy is generally considered a *prima facie* rather than an absolute right. Current debates over privacy generally, and information privacy specifically, are really debates over the limits of personal freedom—that is, the extent to which people are, or should be, entitled to be free from scrutiny and judgment in certain areas of their lives, when there are others who claim to be entitled to prevent them from exercising that freedom. Part of the price we pay for community membership is the sacrifice of some degree of privacy when this is required either to fulfill ourselves as social beings or to further other compelling societal interests. The problem then becomes one of balancing the individual's claim to privacy against the state's claim to regulate conduct for the collective welfare, against the claim of other individuals to exercise their legitimate rights, and against the individual's own need for participation in wider communities.[9]

It is generally conceded that the principle of freedom of information, or the public's "right to know," constitutes a legitimate constraint on the individual's right to information privacy. The public interest in an informed citizenry and an accountable government requires that when the individual's right to privacy becomes an impediment to the realization of the public's right to know, the former must give way to the latter. The question is, how broadly (or narrowly) should the public's interest in personal information be defined? We can accept quite readily that the public interest is served by the disclosure of government-held personal information when it facilitates citizens' oversight of governmental affairs. But is the public interest equally served by the disclosure of personal information for other worthy, though less tangible, ends, for example, to further the purposes of scientific or social research? Put another way, does society's need for knowledge constitute a justifiable restraint on the right to privacy?

Many in the research community would answer in the affirmative, invoking in their defense the principle of academic freedom, or the scholar's "right" to pursue and to communicate knowledge. To the extent that privacy restrictions on government-held personal information would make some studies impossible to perform, they argue that these restrictions intrude on the scholar's right to illuminate unknown regions of human understanding. The conflict between the competing values of individual autonomy and freedom of inquiry triggered by researchers' claims for access to government-held personal information has its roots in the individualist premises of modern liberal society. According to Edward Shils:

> The respect for privacy rests on the appreciation of human dignity, with its high evaluation of individual

self-determination, free from the bonds of prejudice, passion and superstition. In this, the respect for human dignity and individuality shares an historical comradeship with the freedom of scientific inquiry, which is equally precious to modern liberalism. The tension between these values, so essential to each other in so many profoundly important ways, is one of the antinomies of modern liberalism.[10]

This antinomy of modern liberalism has particular relevance for government archivists because a great deal of personal information collected and maintained by government agencies eventually ends up in their custody; leaving them with the unenviable task of reconciling legitimate but conflicting interests—the individual's right to privacy and society's need for knowledge.

The archivists' professional responsibility to ensure a just and equitable balance between these competing interests is dictated by their dual role as public trustees of the records, with a duty to safeguard the privacy interests contained in them, and as communicators of society's documentary memory, with a responsibility to facilitate access to the records that embody it. Striking the appropriate balance between these two responsibilities, however, has proven to be an elusive goal. Archivists' efforts to develop policies and procedures that reflect a proper balance between privacy and research interests have been impeded by a number of factors, among them: a plethora of legal and administrative strictures that are either silent or ambivalent on the question of access for research purposes; the technological complexity of the recordkeeping environments; and, perhaps most debilitatingly, the archivists' general lack of authority (both self-imposed and externally determined) to make access decisions when records containing personal information, particularly sensitive personal information, are involved.

These impediments notwithstanding, archivists are bound by their professional calling to identify, preserve, and make available for use records of enduring value.[11] Before they can make such records available for use, they must understand the administrative, legal, and ethical dimensions of the privacy access debate and its implications for the management of archival records; and they need to translate that knowledge into policies and procedures that will ensure that access to records implicating privacy values is administered in a systematic and equitable manner.

This book is an exploration of the theoretical and practical issues associated with the administration of access to government-held personal information generally and to personal information held in government archives specifically. Its theme is the nature of the balance archivists must strike in negotiating access to such information: how do archivists reconcile research and privacy interests concerning the disclosure of personal information? In situations where the two interests conflict, where does the archivists' professional responsibility lie? In the first three chapters the current debates over access to government-held personal information will be discussed with reference to the moral and legal principles underlying the right to privacy; the emergence of a specific right to information privacy and its embodiment in Canadian and American legislation; as well as the different approaches the two countries have taken to reconciling public and private interests concerning the disclosure of government-held personal information.

In the remaining chapters the particular dilemmas that plague the administration of access to personal information in government archives will be studied in more detail. A number of topics will be addressed: the trends in socio-historical research that have contributed to the growing demand for records containing personal information in government archives; the administrative and legal difficulties archivists encounter in administering access to these records and the various approaches that have been taken to cope with these difficulties; the ethics of disclosing personal information for research purposes and the principles that should guide archivists in making access decisions; and, finally, the policies and practices that will ensure a just and equitable balance between the competing imperatives of individual privacy, on the one hand, and freedom of inquiry on the other.

Notes

1. Samuel Warren and Louis Brandeis, "The Right to Privacy [the implicit made explicit]," *Harvard Law Review* 4 (5) (1890), reprinted in *Philosophical Dimensions of Privacy,* ed. Ferdinand Schoeman (Cambridge, Mass.: Cambridge University Press, 1984), 75-103.
2. Ibid., 77.
3. Raymond Williams, *Keywords: A Vocabulary of Culture and Society* (Glasgow: Fontana, 1976), 203.
4. Ibid., 204.
5. Richard F. Hixson, *Privacy in A Public Society: Human Rights in Conflict* (New York: Oxford University Press, 1987), 47.
6. See, for example, David H. Flaherty, *Privacy in Colonial New England* (Charlottesville, Va.: University of Virginia Press, 1972).
7. Arthur Schafer, "Privacy: A Philosophical Overview," in *Aspects of Privacy Law: Essays in Honour of John M. Sharp,* ed. Dale Gibson (Toronto: Butterworths, 1980), 2.
8. Ibid., 2.
9. Ibid., 19.
10. Edward Shils, "Social Inquiry and the Autonomy of the Individual," in *Social Research Ethics,* ed. Martin Bulmer (New York: Holmes and Meier, 1982), 130.
11. Society of American Archivists, *Planning for the Archival Profession: A Report of the Society of American Archivists Task Force on Goals and Priorities* (Chicago: Society of American Archivists, 1986), vi.

Defining Moral and Legal Zones of Privacy

> Privacy, like an elephant, is more readily recognized than described.
>
> John B. Young
> *Privacy*

If the concept of privacy is, as Young suggests, "more readily recognized than described,"[1] it is equally true that the right to privacy traditionally has been easier to defend than to define. Our modern notion of privacy is linked historically to the emergence, in the eighteenth century, of individual "natural" rights which were considered to be essential to the individual's growth and fulfillment in society. Rousseau exalted privacy as the ground of philosophical truth, for "a man cannot speak the truth about the world unless he cuts himself off from it."[2]

The establishment of individual rights created a political structure in which an individual's right to privacy could be articulated—if only implicitly. It was not until the late nineteenth century, however, that privacy began to emerge as a right distinctive from other individual rights and not until the early 1970s that the philosophical and legal issues underlying the right to privacy became the focus of sustained discussion and debate. The two major obstacles to defining privacy are accurately captured in the 1972 report of a British Government Committee on

Privacy (the Younger Report).[3] First, many of the things we feel the need to preserve from the prying eyes of others are feelings, beliefs, or matters of conduct that are essentially irrational; and second, the scope of privacy is determined largely by the standards and mores of a given society, and these standards are subject to constant change. The Younger Report concluded that "the concept of privacy cannot be satisfactorily defined," citing in support the equally pessimistic conclusions reached by an earlier British Justice Committee on Privacy, which were:

> ... that no purpose would be served by our making yet another attempt at developing an intellectually rigorous analysis. . . . At any given time, there will be certain things which almost everyone will agree ought to be part of the "private" area which people should be allowed to preserve from the intrusion of others, subject only to the overriding interest of the community as a whole where this plainly outweighs the private right. Surrounding this area there will always be a "grey area" on which opinions will differ, and the extent of this grey area, as also that of the central one, is bound to vary from time to time.[4]

These conclusions notwithstanding, the enormous growth of the institutions and devices of communications has made mandatory the need to define privacy and to characterize its moral and legal dimensions. Debates over the legitimacy of the right to privacy typically focus on three essential questions: how do we define privacy? On what moral grounds can we defend a "right to privacy"? And, finally, to what extent is this moral right supported in law?

Privacy has been defined by some as a claim or right of individuals to noninterference, articulated concisely as "the right to be let alone."[5] According to this definition, privacy is synonymous with negative liberty. The equation has some validity since the standard cases of invasion of privacy commonly take the form of coercive intrusions upon the individual and relate to such issues as theft, trespass, copyright, and defamation of character. Nonetheless, the definition is flawed inasmuch as it lacks the distinctiveness necessary for the phrase to be useful in more than a conclusory sense. "The right to be let alone" covers almost any conceivable complaint a citizen could make, and a great many examples of not letting people alone cannot readily be described as invasions of privacy. The definition is at the same time too narrow since it is possible to violate a person's privacy without any coercion or interference with freedom of action. Surveillance of various kinds can take place without our knowledge—wiretapping or computer-matching are just two examples—and in each case we suffer a loss of privacy, notwithstanding the fact that we are not coerced and our freedom of action, thought, and expression has not been interfered with. In some instances the negative liberty attaching to the right to be let alone may even conflict with the right to privacy. H. J. McCloskey, for example, argues that it may be necessary, in order to protect an individual's right to privacy, to interfere with the liberty of others to spy upon that person or to publish information about that person.[6]

The right to make personal decisions without interference by the state constitutes yet another variation on the theme of privacy as the right to be let alone. This interpretation has been applied in at least two U.S. Supreme Court decisions which have determined that, for the purposes of American law, the right to privacy includes the right of a married couple to use contraceptives[7] and the right of a woman to have an abortion prior to the seventh month of pregnancy, with the approval of a doctor.[8] In such cases, the concept of privacy is extended to protect individuals' liberty of actions and autonomy from state regulation of certain intimate aspects of their lives.

There are at least three problems with this interpretation of privacy. First, it excludes all claims that are unrelated to highly personal decisions, such as an individual's unwillingness to be "on file" in a central data bank. Second, to define privacy as noninterference with private actions is to restrict the context in which we can speak about important issues relating to state interference with individual action, issues that may be more effectively addressed under the umbrella concept of liberty of action.[9] Finally, to treat privacy as a right of noninterference presumes that privacy is morally significant; yet the definition fails to identify precisely what it is about privacy that is so significant.

Yet another variation on privacy as a claim or entitlement is one that takes information control rather than noninterference as its essential characteristic. Alan Westin's definition of privacy as "the claim of individuals, groups, or institutions to determine for themselves when, how, and to what extent information about them is communicated to others"[10] is the most frequently cited in this regard, and its influence on the study of privacy has been enormous. Other proponents of the control type definition include Richard Parker, who defines privacy as control over who senses us;[11] Charles Fried, who defines it as "the control we have over information about ourselves;"[12] and Arthur Miller, who identifies privacy as "the individual's ability to control the circulation of information relating to him."[13]

The advantage of the information control definition of privacy is that it identifies clearly the interest involved when people resist surveillance or monitoring of their affairs, that interest being the desire of individuals and groups to disclose what they are doing on their own terms and to whom they choose.[14] It has, nevertheless, serious limitations that become apparent when the different senses of the definition are examined. According to one sense of the definition—the "weak sense" definition of control—a voluntary disclosure does not involve loss of privacy because such a disclosure would be considered an exercise of control, rather than a loss of it. Edward Shils defines privacy in a way that reinforces this notion: "Privacy exists where the persons whose actions engender or become the objects of information retain possession of that information, and any flow outward of that information from the persons to whom it refers . . . occurs on the initiative of its possessors."[15] Control over the decision to disclose information, rather than control over the amount of information others actually have, is emphasized here. The alternative, "strong sense," definition of control would view voluntary disclosure as a loss of control because the person who discloses loses the power to prevent others from further disseminating the information.

Both the "weak" and "strong" sense definitions of information control are problematic. The first claims too little, because individuals can have control over whether to disclose personal information and yet not control the information and access others have to them through other means. The second claims too much because it may indicate a loss of privacy when there is only a threat of such loss. Moreover, in both senses of the definition, the equation of privacy with the right of individuals to control the flow of information about themselves does not establish whether they are in fact known by others through other means.

A more serious concern with control definitions of privacy is that they situate the essence of privacy in the ability to choose it and see that the choice is respected; the power of choice is emphasized rather than the way in which such power should be exercised, thereby preempting important moral questions about when and why losses of privacy are undesirable. There are losses of privacy that have nothing to do with losses of control, and the reasons we value privacy may have nothing to do with whether an individual has in fact chosen it. If privacy is defined as a form of control it prohibits us from criticizing how that control—to choose privacy or not to choose it—is exercised.[16]

Ruth Gavison has suggested an alternative characterization of privacy, one that identifies it with a state or condition of limited access to a person. To define privacy in a way that does not preempt questions about its moral status, Gavison contends, we should begin by identifying the loss of privacy. [17] Such a loss occurs as others obtain information about us, pay attention to us, or gain access to us. If we translate these losses of privacy into a definition, privacy then becomes "the extent to which we are known to others; the extent to which we are the subject of others' attention; and the extent to which others have physical access to us." [18]

This characterization of privacy is perhaps the most useful one because it is both coherent and distinctive. The neutral definition suggests a complex of three independent and irreducible elements: secrecy, anonymity, and solitude. [19] Although each element can function independently within its own self-contained area of privacy concern, the definition is nevertheless coherent because all three elements are part of the same notion of accessibility. The concern for secrecy, or the amount of information known about an individual, relates to information gathering practices; the concern for anonymity, or the attention paid to an individual, refers to losses of privacy that result when we become the subject of others' attention, either by direct or indirect observation; and the concern for solitude, to physical access: here the concern is not that more information has been obtained, nor that more attention has been drawn to us, but that our "spatial aloneness" has been encroached on.[20]

It is not only the definition of privacy that must satisfy the "coherence" and "distinctiveness" criteria; the moral defense of privacy also hinges on its status as a distinct and coherent right. Debates over the status of privacy as a moral right typically focus on two questions concerning the reducibility of privacy to other interests or rights. First, is there something coherent, that is, fundamental, integrated, and unique, about the concerns commonly grouped together as privacy issues, or are those concerns only randomly associated? Second, is there something morally distinctive about privacy, or can privacy claims be defended by the same moral principles on which we base our defense of other values?[21] The range of privacy concerns is remarkably wide and diverse, a fact that has led some critics to assume a skeptical position with respect to its distinct and coherent moral value.

Critics such as Judith Jarvis Thomson maintain that what we call "the right to privacy" is a catch-all phrase disguising a cluster of independent rights lacking a com-

Defining Moral and Legal Zones of Privacy   15

mon foundation. "... the right to privacy is itself a cluster of rights ... it is not a distinct cluster of rights but itself intersects with the cluster of rights which the right over the person consists in and also with the cluster of rights which owning property consists in."[22] The right to privacy fails to constitute a significant moral category in its own right, Thomson maintains, because what needs to be said about privacy can be best expressed without reference to privacy at all. A person's right to privacy is violated only if another more basic right has been violated.

In a similar vein, William Prosser refutes the notion that privacy constitutes a distinct right by arguing, from common law interpretations of privacy invasion (i.e., tort law), that privacy law protects against four distinct kinds of invasion—intrusion upon a person's seclusion, solitude, or into one's private affairs; public disclosure of embarrassing private facts; public disclosure of a private person which places the person in a false light in the public eye; and appropriation, for one's own advantage, of another's name or likeness. These four types of invasion relate, in turn, to different interests of the plaintiff in reputation, emotional tranquility, and proprietary gain. According to Prosser, these "are tied together by the common name [privacy], but otherwise have almost nothing in common except that each represents an interference with the right of the plaintiff ... 'to be let alone'."[23] Prosser concludes from his analysis of tort law that the interests we seek to protect when we judge something private are not distinctively privacy interests; rather, they are the ordinary kinds of interests which many laws, having nothing to do with privacy, aim at ensuring.[24] Such a conclusion presumes, of course, that privacy concepts arising from adjudication will be coherent when there is no guarantee that this will be the case, particularly when the theoretical basis underlying the concept of privacy has never been settled in common law.

The argument that there is something distinctive and coherent in claims to privacy is based on the belief "that something unique about human moral or social character is lost in reductive accounts [such as Thomson's or

Prosser's]—something that transcends the particular cases being analyzed."[25] The notion that privacy is connected in a specific and profound way with human moral character was first articulated by Samuel Warren and Louis Brandeis,[26] who advocated a general right to privacy based on the principle of "inviolate personality." Edward Bloustein[27] has extrapolated the notion of inviolate personality in order to refute William Prosser's claim that privacy concerns are reducible to interests in emotional tranquility, reputation, and proprietary gain. In Bloustein's view, "inviolate personality" embraces individual dignity and integrity, personal uniqueness and individual autonomy; it is respect for these values—all aspects of human dignity—which provides the ground on which an individual's right to privacy is claimed.[28]

Bloustein's assertion that the coherence of privacy rests on the fact that all invasions are violations of human dignity has been challenged by a number of critics, among them, Ruth Gavison: "We may well be concerned with invasions of privacy, at least in part, because they are violations of dignity. But there are ways to offend dignity and personality that have nothing to do with privacy."[29] Being forced to line up for food at a foodbank in order to feed oneself or one's children is one example of an affront to human dignity that has little to do with privacy.

Other defenses of privacy as a moral right stress its role in providing individuals with the opportunity to maintain important interpersonal relationships and intimate parts of life. Charles Fried and James Rachels, for example, argue[30] that privacy provides the necessary context for the development of trust, love, and friendship because, "if we cannot control who has access to us, sometimes including and sometimes excluding people, then we cannot control the patterns of behavior we need to adopt . . . or the kinds of relations with other people that we will have."[31] Privacy is a necessary precondition for the creation and maintenance of different kinds of social relationships, because, "we act differently if we believe we are being observed. If we can never be sure whether or not we are being watched and listened to, all our actions will be altered and our very character will change."[32] The psychological need for a protected zone of privacy is revealed starkly in Erving Goffman's analysis of prisons and mental institutions:

> ... beginning with admission a kind of contaminative exposure occurs. On the outside, the individual can hold objects of self-feeling—such as his body, his immediate actions, his thoughts and some of his possessions—clear of contact with alien and contaminating things. But in total institutions these territories of self are violated; the boundary that the individual places between his being and the environment is invaded and the embodiments of self profaned.[33]

Goffman's observations confirm the importance of privacy for the development and preservation of personal identity by illuminating the effects of its erosion in "total institutions."

The moral value of privacy can best be understood by reference to its specific functions in promoting the liberty of individuals and of society. First, by limiting others' physical access to us, privacy insulates us from the distracting and inhibiting effects of social life. "Freedom from distraction," Ruth Gavison argues, "is essential for all human activities that require concentration, such as learning, writing, and all forms of creativity;"[34] the tragic life of the child prodigy William James Sidis lends eloquent support to this argument.[35] Freedom from physical access is also a prerequisite for the relaxation and intimacy essential for many kinds of human relationships and provides a necessary shield for intimate relations. Yet another kind of freedom—from censure and ridicule in the early stages of experimentation—is facilitated by privacy.[36] If all our failures were exposed to public view, we would be less likely to take risks and areas of intellectual inquiry would shrink to the predictable and the known; by shielding the individual from such exposure, privacy contributes in another way to learning and creativity.

Another value connected to the function of privacy in promoting liberty is autonomy, defined as "the reflective and critical acceptance of social norms, with obedience based on an independent moral evaluation of their worth."[37] Our freedom to seek moral autonomy—to deliberate and establish opinions without interference or coercion—is dependent on the presence of a certain measure of privacy since, even in a theoretically open and tolerant society, individuals or groups who behave in a manner that deviates from certain norms are subject to hostile treatment.

The liberty promoted by privacy is also important to the formation and maintenance of different kinds of human attachments because privacy enables us to edit and present our different selves to the world. This function is crucial because we project our identity through these various selves and it is through such images of self that human relations are created and maintained.[38] Some privacy critics, notably Richard Wasserstrom and Richard Posner, object to this justification for privacy, arguing that we either act authentically or inauthentically as we present ourselves in various contexts. According to Posner, we have no right to manipulate the opinions that other people hold of us by controlling the information that is known about us.[39] Moreover, Wasserstrom suggests, not revealing information about oneself may be considered presumptively improper because it is morally equivalent to deception.[40] On these grounds, both writers would contend, our wish to present different versions of ourselves in different contexts should not be supported ethically or legally. Such a position, which presumes the existence of an integrated core self, is not well supported by current psychological or social analytic theories, which tend to suggest that there is no core person underlying the various selves we present in different contexts.[41] We always present edited versions of ourselves depending on the situation in which we find ourselves. The question, Ruth Gavison maintains, "is not whether we should edit, but how and by whom the editing should be done."[42]

Arguments that defend privacy on the grounds that it promotes liberty of action are predicated on an assumption that individuals should be permitted a sphere of privacy in which to think and act in ways that might be judged inappropriate or unacceptable if exposed to public scrutiny. The assumption raises an important question concerning the limits of such liberty. Does privacy promote in every case a liberty that we consider desirable or even permissible? The liberty privacy affords is not, generally speaking, problematic in contexts in which we believe we should have few or no norms; for example, in cases where freedom of expression and racial tolerance are involved. The existence of anti-discrimination or freedom of expression laws is not in itself a guarantee that individuals or groups will not be subject to prejudice or pressures to conform. Respect for privacy is a way of enforcing tolerance of others, a necessary compromise between the ideals of social harmony and the limits of human nature.[43]

Privacy also appears to be permissible in contexts in which we question the desirability of certain norms or where no clear consensus on their desirability exists. Although homosexual relations between consenting adults is still illegal in half the American states, the law is rarely enforced, which suggests that the privacy of such relationships is allowed in order to protect the participants from legal sanctions.[44] Other contexts in which we allow privacy to function in this way are when privacy promotes our liberty not to disclose a criminal past in the interests of rehabilitation; or our membership in a dissident political organization as a protection against prejudice or discrimination. In such cases, respect for privacy serves to ease tensions between personal preferences and social norms by permitting the nonenforcement of certain standards.[45] The problem inherent in this particular justification for privacy, Gavison suggests, is that it allows privacy to function in a way that perpetuates the very problems it intends to ease. "If homosexuals are not prosecuted, there is no need to decide whether such conduct between consenting adults in private can constitutionally be prohibited." [46] Similarly, if people only share their independent judgments with like-minded individuals, the opportunity to confront and possibly diminish public hostility never presents itself. Privacy might, in such situations, reduce our incentive to publicly question the desirability of certain social norms.

Our willingness to allow privacy to function in this way will depend, finally, on our judgment concerning the amount of liberty to which individuals are, or should be, entitled. Although it is unlikely that legal and social changes will come about if individuals are unwilling to challenge norms, given the reality of entrenched moral attitudes there should be a presumption in favor of the individual. The individual's right to choose privacy rather than challenge authority is eloquently defended by Ruth Gavison: "If the chance to achieve change in a particular case is small, it seems heartless and naive to argue against the use of privacy . . . if an individual prefers to present a public conformity rather than unconventional autonomy, that is his choice. The least society can do in such cases is respect such a choice." [47]

Privacy not only protects and promotes individual moral autonomy and meaningful human relationships; it also promotes a more pluralistic and tolerant society. Arthur Schafer traces the social value of privacy back to the utilitarian principles first espoused by John Stuart Mill in *On Liberty:*

> As Mill points out, there is a close correlation between the availability of a protected zone of privacy and the individual's ability freely to develop his individuality and creativity. In a society which is frequently intolerant of or hostile to non-conformity, freedom from constant surveillance is an important pre-condition for the development of independent and critically-minded individuals. Diversity and non-conformity will, in turn, promote the vitality and progress of society and contribute thereby to long-run utility.[48]

Privacy is important for democracy because the justification for majority rule and the right to vote rests on the

assumption that citizens should participate in political decisions by forming judgments and establishing choices. If citizens are to exercise their political liberty to the fullest extent, they must have the right to keep private their votes, their political discussions, and their associations. The argument holds equally true for groups. If they are to protect their organizational life, ideological protest movements, unions and a variety of other groups and movements all require what Arthur Schafer calls "a kind of nutritive privacy" with respect to their internal affairs, "
. . . unless individuals and groups have wide scope to formulate and test their ideas without intrusive surveillance by governments, the police or the general public, an essential precondition for an effective democratic society will be destroyed."[49]

A number of social critics allege, with some justification, that we suffer from too much privacy, that it has become an unhealthy obsession of modern liberal society, an indicator of social pathology rather than social health wherein we "seek more and more privacy, and feel more and more alienated when we get it."[50] The excessive stress which liberal ideology places on privacy and the consequent turning away from the public aspects of life, such critics argue, has damaged the tissues of social connection and withered public spiritedness.

The societal ideal that is sometimes invoked implicitly in such criticism is one of universal transparency. Meister Eckhart maintained that "we call him a good man who reveals himself to others and in so doing is of use to them."[51] In a similar vein, Jean-Paul Sartre argued that "transparency must substitute itself at all times for secrecy."[52] He was realistic enough, however, to surmise that such transparency would be achievable only when material want had been eradicated and human relations were no longer fraught with antagonisms, "the day when two men will have no more secrets from one another because they will keep secrets from no one, since the subjective life, just as much as the objective life, will be totally offered, given."[53]

In the world as it presently exists, privacy possesses a paradoxical ability both to facilitate the development of social relationships and to diminish human interaction depending on the way it is incorporated with other social values and embedded in social institutions.[54] Psychologists O. M. Reubhausen and O. G. Brim, Jr., emphasize the dual aspects of privacy when they insist that, "[b]oth of these conflicting needs, in mutually supportive interaction, are essential to the well-being of individuals and institutions, and any definition of privacy, or of private personality, must reflect this plastic duality: sharing and concealment."[55] Individuals must be in some intermediate state—a balance between privacy and interaction—in order to maintain human relations, develop their capacities and sensibilities, create, and, ultimately, to survive. The question that remains is, how effectively does our system of legal jurisprudence in the area of privacy reconcile our competing needs for individual autonomy and social membership?

In both the United States and Canada, a certain measure of privacy has been accorded constitutional protection. Although the word *privacy* does not appear in the American Constitution or in the Bill of Rights, the U. S. Supreme Court has nevertheless specified a legally defensible right to privacy through case by case judicial inclusion and exclusion. The Court has found the constitutional basis for an individual's legal claim to privacy in the Bill of Rights, particularly in the First, Fourth, Fifth, Ninth, and Fourteenth Amendments which address matters relating to individual freedom of association, protection against unreasonable search and seizure and self-incrimination, and the right to due process. In *Griswold v. Connecticut,* which struck down Connecticut's attempt to regulate the use of contraceptive devices, the Court noted that "specific guarantees in the Bill of Rights have penumbras, formed by emanations from those guarantees that help give them life and substance.... [These] create zones of privacy."[56]

Nonetheless, with the exception of the right to associational privacy,[57] the constitutional protection of private zones has been limited, in the United States, to cases involving the abuse of government power by unreasonable searches or in "matters relating to marriage, procreation, contraception, family relationships, and child-bearing and education."[58] In a number of Supreme Court decisions written since 1971, information privacy has been specifically excluded from constitutional protection.[59] The considerably younger Canadian Charter of Rights and Freedoms does not express an explicit commitment to the right of privacy either, although such a right has been inferred from section eight of the Charter which protects individual citizens against unlawful search or seizure.[60]

Although the case law rarely discusses the distinction between the constitutional right to privacy and the common law right, it is generally understood that, whereas the constitution protects individuals from government intrusion into their lives, the common law typically dictates rights that exist between private citizens.[61] The common law right to privacy can be traced to the formal recognition of private property, around which grew a legal system relating to theft, trespass, copyright, and squatter's rights. In British Commonwealth jurisdictions, including Canada, a specific tort of invasion of privacy does not exist.[62] Where the term is used in court decisions granting a legal remedy, it is usually taken to mean that privacy interests intersect with others that the law already recognizes and protects. The causes of action that do protect privacy interests are usually available where privacy and property, reputational, or physical integrity interests have been granted legal protection, for example, in actions involving trespass, nuisance, defamation, appropriation of personality for commercial purposes, and breach of confidence.[63]

In the United States, an explicit recognition of a right to privacy, as a right of personality rather than property, was first articulated by Warren and Brandeis in their 1890 article, "The Right to Privacy," which was published in the *Harvard Law Review.* Warren and Brandeis' plea for the recognition of such a right stemmed from their concern that an individual's private domain was vulnerable to the increasingly intrusive practices of the so-called "yellow press" and that the law did not protect the individual adequately against invasions of privacy resulting from the publication or public dissemination of private information:

> Of the desirability—indeed of the necessity—of some such protection, there can, it is believed, be no doubt. The press is overstepping in every direction the obvious bounds of propriety and of decency. . . . To satisfy a prurient taste the details of sexual relations are spread broadcast in the columns of the daily papers. To occupy the indolent, column upon column is filled with idle gossip, which can only be procured by intrusion upon the domestic circle.[64]

Although laws relating to property, copyright, contract, and breach of confidence had been used in the past to protect privacy interests, Warren and Brandeis believed that the law should explicitly entitle individuals to determine the extent to which their thoughts, sentiments, or emotions—regardless of their commercial or artistic value—become available to the world at large.

The recognition of the moral and spiritual integrity of individuals, rather than simply their material interests, is at the heart of Warren and Brandeis' argument for a specific legal entitlement to privacy: "The intensity and complexity of life, attendant upon advancing civilization, have rendered necessary some retreat from the world . . . so that solitude and privacy have become more essential to the individual." The public dissemination of private facts subjected an individual "to mental pain and distress, far greater than could be inflicted by mere bodily injury."[65] The Warren-Brandeis article is usually credited with leading most American states to recognize a right to recover in tort for the wrongful exposure of private information and for a wide range of other types of invasion. In the court decisions that have recognized a right of privacy since Warren and Brandeis published their defense of it, the original "private facts" tort has undergone some considerable expansion; by 1960, William Prosser could identify four distinct torts commonly labelled invasions of privacy.[66]

Nevertheless, despite the enormous number of claims litigated under the private facts tort, plaintiffs rarely win.[67] The failure of the American common law to protect plaintiffs is attributable partly to the inherent first amendment dilemma it presents by treating truthful speech as tortious. Some commentators have gone so far as to suggest that "the Warren-Brandeis contribution has actually had a pernicious influence on modern tort law because it created a cause of action that, however formulated, cannot coexist with constitutional protections for freedom of speech and press."[68] In order to protect free speech, courts have had to create numerous defenses of it when it has conflicted with privacy interests and narrow the scope of the privacy tort in order to allow a great deal of personal information to circulate without penalty.

Among the constraints placed on an individual's ability to claim a right of privacy under the private facts tort and seek civil remedies through the courts are: the facts disclosed about a person must be of a private nature and not of things that a person has done in public or which are a matter of public record; the disclosure itself must be public, not private, in nature; the matters made public must be ones that would be "offensive and objectionable to a reasonable person of ordinary sensibilities;" and the right of privacy, in most circumstances, can only be claimed by living individuals. Even if a claim meets all these requirements, a defendant may defeat the action by showing that the public has a legitimate interest in the disclosed facts.

Moreover, although the private facts tort has been applied in court decisions protecting individuals against the misuse of information in data banks,[69] the judicial emphasis on a public disclosure makes the tort difficult to apply in such cases. In the context of computerized information, invasions of privacy are most likely to occur when personal information is exchanged between record-keeping organizations; it can then be used in ways that may damage an individual without the information ever being disclosed publicly. Although there are cases in which victims learn that their privacy has been invaded because the information that has been acquired about them is used in a public trial—the break-in of the office of Daniel Ellsberg's psychiatrist is a notable example[70]—in most situations there is no need to use the information publicly, and victims will not be able to complain about an invasion simply out of ignorance that it has occurred. This lack of awareness may encourage such invasions, Ruth Gavison suggests, since "deterrence depends at least partly on the probability of detection."[71]

The requirement that the information revealed be private presents another problem, since a court's treatment of particular facts will depend on its interpretation of the "reasonable person" standard; court decisions have not been consistent on this point.[72] Further, Arthur Miller suggests, the emphasis on community standards rather than on a fixed norm may exercise an insidious effect on the public's (and the court's) perception of privacy:

> just as constant exposure to scenes of war and squalor have caused many to grow callous about human life and the destruction of the environment, the public may lose its sense of the private if large-scale transfers and dissemination of personal information become common. . . . [Moreover] [i]tems of information that individually would be considered private may lose that status when intermingled in a computer file with quantities of public information.[73]

Miller fears that constant intrusions on personal privacy may numb the public's response to violations of it and, in the long run, render a "reasonable person" incapable of distinguishing between public and private information.

The most glaring deficiency in the existing common law structure of privacy is that it fails to allow individuals to participate in decisions relating to personal information about them. As Miller points out: "It makes no sense to rely on the victim's right to bring suit against those who have injured him when he is not informed of the source of his injury—or, in some cases, he remains unaware of the fact that he has been damaged."[74] Even in those cases where invasion of privacy can be proven, for example, invasion of privacy through publication, legal proceedings are lengthy, costly and, more importantly, involve additional losses of privacy, as Ruth Gavison makes clear: "The law, as one of the most public mechanisms society has developed, is completely out of place in most of the contexts in which privacy is deemed valuable."[75] For the genuine victim of a loss of privacy, damages and even injunctions are "remedies of despair."[76]

It is apparent from the above that constitutional and common law protections of privacy do not always reflect fully or protect adequately the need individuals have for privacy in their daily lives. The law's commitments to other societal interests—in free speech, law enforcement, or public health and safety—must sometimes override the interest in privacy. But there are other, less obvious reasons for the law's limitations in the area of privacy protection. Many of the modern concerns with actual or potential losses of privacy arise, not from the public disclosure of private information, but from the development of technology that allows for the exchange of computerized information and the development of data banks. Advances in the technology of surveillance, recording, storage, and retrieval of information have made it either impossible or extremely costly for individuals to protect the same level of privacy that was once enjoyed.

If we consider Ruth Gavison's earlier characterization of privacy as, "the extent to which we are known to others [secrecy]; the extent to which we are the subject of others' attention [anonymity]; and the extent to which others have physical access to us [solitude] . . . ", it is clear that modern concerns over losses of privacy relate for the most part to secrecy, or the amount of information known about an individual, which have emerged in response to situations created by information gathering practices ignored in traditional interpretations of invasion of privacy.

In a 1978 report on privacy, the Australian Law Reform Commission equated the need for information privacy with:

> ... the need for proper respect for the autonomy of the individual. To deny the individual the ability to control, to an appropriate extent, his relationships with others in the community is to compromise his autonomy. In the context of personal information, the individual's claim to privacy is therefore a claim to control, to an appropriate extent, the way that others in the community perceive him. The way that personal information about individuals is collected, used and disclosed is a matter for privacy concern.[77]

The Commission's observations are indicative of the growing recognition on the part of legislators that citizens have a need for, and a right to, information privacy. Most would now agree that, to make privacy law more just and effective in the area of information privacy, it must focus on, "identifying (preferably by statute) those exchanges of information that warrant protection at their point of origin, rather than continuing its current, capricious course of imposing liability only if the material is ultimately disseminated to the public at large."[78] The last fifteen years have witnessed the emergence, in most western countries, of data protection legislation which focuses on the collection, use, and disclosure of personal information, mainly by government agencies. The bureaucratic and technological imperatives that have created the demand for data protection and its codification in American and Canadian federal privacy laws will be examined in the next chapter.

Notes

1. John B. Young, ed., *Privacy* (New York: Wiley, 1978), 2.

2. Jean Marie Goulemot, "Literary Practices: Publicizing the Private," *Passions of the Renaissance*, vol. 3 of *A History of Private Life*, ed. Roger Chartier (Cambridge, Mass.: Harvard University Press, 1989), 389.

3. *Report of the Committee on Privacy*, under the Chairmanship of the Rt. Hon. Kenneth Younger (London: Her Majesty's Stationery Office, 1972).

4. British Section of the International Commission of Jurists, "Privacy and the Law," quoted in *Report of the Committee on Privacy*, 17-18.

5. The notion of a right "to be let alone" was first advanced in Thomas M. Cooley, "The right to be let alone," *Torts* 29 (2nd ed. 1888).

6. H. J. McCloskey, "Privacy and the Right to Privacy," *Philosophy* 55 (1980): 17-38.

7. *Griswold v. Connecticut* (1965) 85 S. Ct. 1678.

8. *Roe vs. Wade* (1973) 410 U. S. 113 (U.S.S.C.).

9. Ruth Gavison, "Privacy and the Limits of the Law," *Yale Law Review* 89 (3) (Jan. 1980): 439.

10. Alan Westin, *Privacy and Freedom* (New York: Atheneum, 1967), 7.

11. Richard Parker, "A Definition of Privacy," *Rutgers Law Review* 27 (1974): 275-96.

12. Charles Fried, *An Anatomy of Values: Problems of Personal and Social Choice* (Cambridge, Mass.: Harvard University Press, 1970), 140.

13. Arthur Miller, *The Assault on Privacy* (Ann Arbor: University of Michigan Press, 1971), 25.

14. Arthur Schafer, "Privacy: A Philosophical Overview," *Aspects of Privacy Law: Essays in Honour of John M. Sharp*, ed. Dale Gibson (Toronto: Butterworths, 1980), 9.

15. Edward Shils, "Privacy: Its Constitution and Vicissitudes," *Law and Contemporary Problems* 31 (Spring 1966): 282.

16. For a more detailed analysis of the "weak" and "strong" sense definitions of control, see Ruth Gavison, "Privacy and the Limits of the Law," 426-28.

17. Gavison, "Privacy and Limits of Law," 421-471.

18. Ibid., 423.

19. Ibid., 434.

20. Ibid., 433.

21. Ferdinand Schoeman, "Privacy: Philosophical Dimensions of the Literature," *Philosophical Dimensions of Privacy*, ed. Ferdinand Schoeman (New York: Cambridge University Press, 1984), 5.

22. Judith Jarvis Thomson, "The Right to Privacy," *Philosophy and Public Affairs* 4 (4) (Summer 1975): 306. For refutations of Thomson's view, see Thomas Scanlon, "Thomson on Privacy," *Philosophy and Public Affairs* 4 (4) (Summer 1975): 315-22; and James Rachels, "Why Privacy is Important," *Philosophy and Public Affairs* 4 (4) (Summer 1975): 323-33.

23. William L. Prosser, "Privacy [a legal analysis]," *California Law Review* 48 (3) (August 1960): 389.

24. See also Frederick Davis, "What Do We Mean by 'Right to Privacy'?" *South Dakota Law Review* 4 (1959): 1-24; and Richard A. Posner, "An Economic Theory of Privacy," in *Philosophical Dimensions of Privacy,* 333-45.

25. Schoeman, "Privacy: Philosophical Dimensions," 6.

26. Samuel D. Warren and Louis D. Brandeis, "The Right to Privacy [the implicit made explicit]," *Harvard Law Review* 4 (5) (1890) reprinted in *Philosophical Dimensions of Privacy,* 75-103.

27. Edward J. Bloustein, "Privacy as an Aspect of Human Dignity: An Answer to Dean Prosser," *New York University Law Review* 39 (December 1964): 962-1007.

28. The notion that privacy is linked in a fundamental way with human dignity, or respect for persons, is also explored by Stanley Benn in "Privacy, Freedom and Respect for Persons," *Nomos XIII: Privacy,* ed. J. R. Pennock and J. W. Chapman (New York: Atherton Press, 1971), 1-26.

29. Gavison, "Privacy and Limits of Law," 438.

30. See Charles Fried, "Privacy," *Yale Law Journal* 77 (1968): 484-85; Rachels, "Why Privacy is Important," 323-33.

31. Rachels, "Why Privacy is Important," 331.

32. Hubert Humphrey, Foreword, *The Intruders: The Invasion of Privacy by Government and Industry,* by Edward V. Long (New York: Frederick A. Praeger, 1967), viii.

33. Erving Goffman, *Asylums: Essays on the Social Situation of Mental Patients and Other Inmates* (New York: Doubleday, 1968), 23.

34. Davison, "Privacy and Limits of Law," 447.

35. William James Sidis was an extraordinarily gifted child who graduated from Harvard at the age of 15. Throughout his childhood, he was subjected to the unrelenting scrutiny of the press who treated him as a kind of freak. Although it was widely predicted that Sidis would become a world-renowned mathematician, instead he retreated from the painful glare of publicity surrounding him and became a file clerk and collector of streetcar transfers. Years later, he became the subject of a *New Yorker* article written by James Thurber, who described Sidis as neu-

rotic and maladjusted. In an ensuing lawsuit for invasion of privacy initiated by Sidis, the Second Circuit Court of Appeals ruled that, while the story was ruthless, the once famous Sidis was not entitled to reclaim a right to privacy with the passage of time. In a recent biography of Sidis, Amy Wallace revealed that it was the torment of public exposure, not his parents' pressure to excel, which stifled Sidis's creative intellect in adulthood and caused his apparent unhappiness. See Amy Wallace, *The Prodigy* (New York: E. P. Dutton, 1986).
    36. Gavison, "Privacy and Limits of Law," 448.
    37. Ibid., 449.
    38. Ibid., 450.
    39. Richard A. Posner, "An Economic Theory of Privacy," *Philosophical Dimensions of Privacy*, 333-345.
    40. Richard Wasserstrom, "Privacy: Some Arguments and Assumptions," *Philosophical Law: Authority, Equality, Adjudication, Privacy*, ed. Richard Bronough (Westport, Conn.: Greenwood Press, 1978), 148-66.
    41. See, for example, Walter Mischel, *Personality and Assessment* (New York: John Wiley, 1968); and Erving Goffman, *The Presentation of Self in Everyday Life* (Garden City, N. Y.: Doubleday, 1959).
    42. Gavison, "Privacy and Limits of Law," 454.
    43. Ibid., 452.
    44. However, the Supreme Court has refused to declare antisodomy laws unconstitutional. See, for example, *Doe v. Commonwealth*, 403 F. Supp. 1199 (E.D. Va. 1975), aff'd mem., 425 U.S. 901 (1976); *Bowers v. Hardwick*, 85-140 (June 30, 1986).
    45. Gavison, "Privacy and Limits of Law," 452.
    46. Ibid., 452.
    47. Ibid., 453.
    48. Schafer, "Privacy: A Philosophical Overview," 15.
    49. Ibid., 14.
    50. Philip Slater, *The Pursuit of Loneliness*, cited in Schafer, "Privacy: A Philosophical Overview," 18.
    51. Cited in Sissela Bok, *Secrets: On the Ethics of Concealment and Revelation* (New York: Vintage, 1983), 17.
    52. Ibid.
    53. Ibid.
    54. Schafer, "Privacy: A Philosophical Overview," 19.
    55. O. M. Reubhausen and Orville Brim, Jr., "Privacy and Behavioral Research," *American Psychologist* 21 (1966): 426.
    56. See *Griswold v. Connecticut*, 318 U.S. 479 (1965) at 484.

57. See *NAACP v. Alabama*, 357 U.S. 449 (1958) (Supreme Court ruling that an Alabama law which required that the National Association for the Advancement of Colored People turn over to the state its membership and officer lists in order to be recognized as an out-of-state corporation was unconstitutional). See also *Bates v. City of Little Rock*, 361 U.S. 516 (1960).

58. Cited in *Paul v. Davis,* 424 U.S. 693, 713 (1976).

59. See, for example, *Paul v. Davis,* 424 U.S. 693 (1976) (individual's claim that his personal reputation had been damaged when police circulated his name on a list of suspected shoplifters dismissed); *Whalen v. Roe,* 429 U.S. 589 (1976) (a state's sophisticated use of computerized information systems ruled not to raise a constitutional objection).

60. See *R. v. Dyment,* December 8, 1988, 89 N.R. 249 [1988] 2 S.C.R. 417, 45 C.C.C. (3d) 244, 66 C.R. (3d) 348 (a police officer's taking of a blood sample without a warrant or the consent of appellant after a traffic accident constitutes unlawful seizure). The Supreme Court ruled that "Section 8 is concerned not only with the protection of property but also with the protection of the privacy interests of individuals from search or seizure. . . . The use of an individual's blood or other bodily substances confided to others for medical purposes for uses other than such purposes seriously violates the personal autonomy of the individual. The seizure here infringed upon all the spheres of privacy—spatial, physical and informational."

61. See Diane L. Zimmerman, "Requiem for a Heavyweight: A Farewell to Warren and Brandeis's Privacy Tort," *Cornell Law Review* 68 (6) (1983): 297-99. The distinction between the constitutional and common law right to privacy has been made in, for example, *Birnbaum v. United States,* 588 F.2d 319, 326 n.14, 327 n.17 (2d Cir. 1978) (suggesting a distinction between common law and constitutional privacy claims); *Drake v. Covington County Bd. of Education,* 317 F. Supp. 974, 980 (M.D. Ala. 1974) (Johnson, C. J. not concurring) (The Warren-Brandeis common law right of privacy not constitutionally based); *Mimms v. Philadelphia Newspapers, Inc.,* 352 F. Supp. 862, 865 n.5 (E.D. Pa. 1972) (distinguishing the right to be free from unwanted publicity from constitutional privacy cases). See also *Bivens v. Six Unknown Named Agents,* 403 U.S. 391-92 (1971) (Fourth Amendment against unlawful search "operates as a limitation upon the exercise of federal power regardless of whether the State in whose jurisdiction that power is exercised would prohibit or penalize the identical act if engaged in by a private citizen.")

62. Provincial legislators in Newfoundland, Manitoba, Saskatchewan and British Columbia have created a statutory tort of invasion of privacy. There may also be a basis for a right of action for invasion of privacy under Article 1053 of the Quebec Civil Code.
63. Peter Burns, "Privacy and the Common Law: A Tangled Skein Unravelling?" *Aspects of Privacy Law: Essays in Honour of John M. Sharp* (Toronto: Butterworths, 1980), 24.
64. Warren and Brandeis, "Right to Privacy," *Philosophical Dimensions of Privacy,* 76-77.
65. Ibid., 77.
66. These included appropriation of another person's name or likeness for personal advantage; intrusion upon a person's solitude or into a person's private affairs; public disclosure of embarrassing private facts about a person; or, publicity that places a person in a false light in the public eye. See Prosser, "Privacy [a legal analysis]," 383-423.
67. In a survey of state law, Diane L. Zimmerman "found fewer than 18 cases in which a plaintiff was either awarded damages or found to have stated a cause of action to withstand a motion for summary judgment or a motion to dismiss." See Zimmerman, "Requiem for a Heavyweight," 293, n.5.
68. Ibid., 293. The issue of reconciling privacy and free speech has been explored by, for example, Edward Bloustein, "Privacy, Tort Law, and the Constitution: Is Warren and Brandeis' Tort Petty and Unconstitutional as Well?" *Texas Law Review* 46 (1968): 611-29; Marc A. Franklin, "A Constitutional Problem in Privacy Protection: Legal Inhibitions on Reporting of Fact," *Stanford Law Review* 16 (1963): 107-48; Prosser, "Privacy [a legal analysis]": 383-423.
69. See, for example, *Senogles v. Security Benefit Life Insurance Co.,* 217 Kan. 438, 536 P.2d 1358 (1975) (insurance company sued for submitting plaintiff's health data to organization that evaluates insurance risks); *Munsell v. Ideal Food Stores,* 208 Kan. 909, 494 P.2d 1063 (1972) (plaintiff sued employer for submitting to plaintiff's union a "confession" of wrongdoing on job); *Klump v. Schwegmann Bros. Giant Supermarkets, Inc.,* 376 So. 2d 514 (La. Ct. App. 1979) (invasion of privacy claim based on communication by defendant of information to plaintiff's employer); *Claspill v. Craig,* 586 S.W.2d 458 (Mo. Ct. App. 1979) (privacy claim against union that publicized resignation of certain members).

70. The break-in of Ellsberg's psychiatrist's office was revealed during the Watergate hearings. See *New York Times*, 28 April 1973: 1.
71. Gavison, "Privacy and Limits of Law," 458.
72. See Zimmerman, "Requiem for a Heavyweight," 299-300, n.32.
73. Miller, *Assault on Privacy,* 181.
74. Ibid., 189.
75. Gavison, "Privacy and Limits of Law," 459.
76. Ibid., 458.
77. [Australian] Law Reform Commission *Report No. 22: Privacy,* vol. 2 (Canberra: Australian Government Publishing Service, 1983), 78.
78. Zimmerman, "Requiem for a Heavyweight," 362-63.

Living for the Record

The Individual, the State, and the Emergence of a Right to Information Privacy

> As every man goes through life he fills in a number of forms for the record, each containing a number of questions. . . . There are thus hundreds of little threads radiating from every man, millions of threads in all. If those threads were suddenly to become visible, the whole sky would look like a spider's web, and if they materialized like rubber bands, buses and trams and even people would lose the ability to move and the wind would be unable to carry torn-up newspapers or autumn leaves along the streets of the city.
>
> Aleksandr Solzhenitsyn
> *Cancer Ward*

In *The Politics of Privacy,* James Rule argues that contemporary concerns over privacy mainly "result from the demands for personal information by powerful but more or less distant social entities,"[1] such as governments. A significant manifestation of the threat to information privacy is the benign surveillance power afforded by the maintenance of personal records by government institutions and agencies. Recordkeeping has been for centuries a tool of public administration, and its primary purpose to provide a mechanism for the social and political control of individual behavior.[2] The rise of the modern welfare state in the 1930s brought with it an enormous increase in the amount of personal information available in public recordkeeping systems. As society has become increasingly urban and anonymous, and as computer technologies have taken hold, recordkeeping systems have expanded in their capacity to store personal information.

The theme of privacy as a right against surveillance makes its appearance early in recorded history. John Curtis Raines traces it back to the book of Genesis when God resisted the power of gazing upon the nakedness of Adam and Eve. "Yahweh God made clothes out of skins for the man and his wife, and they put them on."[3] This passage, Raines suggests, can be read today as, "a warning written over man's interaction with his fellows of the right of self-defense against the imperialism of relentless inquiry, against all watching that would everywhere follow, probe, and hold a person within its sovereign gaze."[4] Historically, the power of "relentless inquiry" has been claimed and exercised by the state, through various mechanisms of surveillance, in the interest of "administering" the lives of its citizens. The gradual emergence of state surveillance, its abusive effects on individual rights to privacy, and the legislative strategies that have been devised to reduce those effects will be examined in this chapter.

In classical Greek thought, the division between public and private—between activities related to a common world and those related to the maintenance of life—stood as a self-evident and axiomatic assumption.[5] The public sphere was the realm of common political activity which directed itself toward the public welfare; the private sphere was synonymous with the household or family realm, and it revolved around the fundamental maintenance of life—food, clothing and shelter. But in the sixteenth, seventeenth, and eighteenth century, the traditional boundary separating the private from the public realm was gradually redrawn in response to three critical developments: the Protestant Reformation and Catholic Counter-Reformation, which demanded of believers greater inward piety and more intimate forms of devotion; the spread of literacy, which emancipated individuals from the old bonds that had attached them to the community in a culture based on speech and gesture; and the new role of the state, which was increasingly taking in hand matters that had hitherto remained beyond its reach.[6]

During the Renaissance, a conceptual shift in political thinking began to take place which altered fundamentally the relationship between the individual and the state and blurred irrevocably the hitherto apparent distinction between the public and private spheres. It was around this time, according to the social critic Michel Foucault, that the household and its method of organization came under the scrutiny of political theorists and treatise writers who found in it both a useful metaphor and an adaptable model for the state. Toward the middle of the sixteenth century, new links between the state—which formed itself around the great territorial monarchies that arose in Europe from the fragments of feudal estates—and the individual—whose spiritual welfare became a political issue in the Reformation and Counter-Reformation—gave rise to a new type of political reflection.[7] A series of treatises on the "art of government" began to appear which introduced, for the first time, detailed analyses of the most efficient means of introducing government, meaning economy and order, from the state at the top down through all aspects of political and social life.

The treatises referred directly to the "governing of a household, souls, children, a province, a convent, a religious order, or a family," and political reflection extended to embrace virtually every aspect of human activity, "from the smallest stirrings of the soul to the largest military manoeuvers of the army."[8] Each activity was scrutinized in order to determine the most economical method by which it could be carried out. "The art of government," Foucault argues,

> [was] concerned with how to introduce economy that is the correct manner of managing individuals, goods and wealth within the family . . . how to introduce this meticulous attention of the father towards his family, into the management of the state.[9]

This new approach to political thinking severed the traditionally fundamental link between the sovereign and a territory, substituting for it a complex relationship of individuals and things in which:

> the things which the government [was] to be concerned about [were] men, but men in their relations, their links, their imbrication with those other things which [were] wealth, resources, means of subsistence, the territory with its specific qualities, climate, irrigation . . . men in their relation to other kinds of things which [were] customs, habits, ways of doing and thinking, etc.; lastly, men in their relation to that other kind of things which [were] accidents and misfortunes such as famine, epidemics, death, etc.[10]

These academic treatises on the art of government can be linked to the rise and growth of centralized state administrative apparatuses from the middle of the sixteenth century onward. By the seventeenth century, this new political rationality had given birth to "statistics," the science of the state, which measured "the different elements, dimensions and factors of the state's power."[11]

As the life process of the population itself became a central concern of the state, a new regime of power—what Foucault has termed "bio-power"—was instituted. Bio-power "brought life and its mechanisms into the realm of explicit calculations."[12] In the middle to late eighteenth century, bio-power fused around two distinct poles: the human species and the human body. According to Foucault, "for the first time in history, scientific categories (species, population, fertility, and so forth), rather than juridical ones, became the object of systematic, sustained political attention and intervention." At the same time, the human body began to be approached "as an object to be manipulated and controlled."[13]

Around this objectification of the body emerged a new "disciplinary technology," a set of procedures directed toward the molding of a docile body and mind. Adopted in a variety of institutional settings—workshops, schools, prisons, and hospitals, for example—this disciplinary technology used drills, physical training, the standardizing of actions over time, and the control of physical space to accomplish its ends. The Panopticon, conceived by Jeremy Bentham in 1791 as the model for a "scientific" prison, was a significant manifestation of disciplinary technology as theory and praxis. Essentially a circular prison, the Panopticon consisted of an annular building surrounding an observation tower. Built into the tower were wide windows that opened out onto the inner side of the ring defined by the annular building which was, in turn, divided into cells; each cell extended the width of the building and possessed two windows: one on the inside, corresponding to the windows of the tower; the other, on the outside, allowing the light to cross the cell from one end to the other. To understand the significance of the design, Foucault explains:

> All that is needed ... is to place a supervisor in a central tower and to shut up in each cell a madman, a patient, a condemned man, a worker or a schoolboy. By the effect of backlighting, one can observe from the tower, standing out precisely against the light, the small captive shadows in the cells of the periphery. They are like so many cages, so many small theatres, in which each actor is alone, perfectly individualized and constantly visible. The panoptic mechanism arranges spatial unities that make it possible to see constantly and recognize immediately.... Visibility is a trap.[14]

The Panopticon is a useful metaphor for the behaviorist sensibility that permeated the Age of Reason. Its essential point, expressed architecturally, was to effect a radical separation between the observer and the observed and to render the latter permanently visible through a schema of generalized surveillance.

Although Bentham's scheme was never fully implemented, its development is crucial to our understanding of the period because it demonstrated that "in the eighteenth century... such a form of power [was] possible and desirable."[15] A self-contained rationality accompanied the panoptic technology, one geared to efficiency and productivity and thus capable of service in a variety of settings. Throughout the remainder of the eighteenth century and into the nineteenth century, the mechanisms of discipline embodied in panopticism—where the powerless were exposed and power lay in the relentless invisible gaze which studied them—gradually extended their reach to broader and broader segments of the population. By the end of the nineteenth century, Foucault suggests, the possibility of knowledge about and control over the most minute aspects of behavior in the name of the population's welfare existed in principle, although it was not fully realized: "Precise dossiers enabl[ed] the authorities to fix individuals in a web of objective codification. . . . This accumulation of documentation [made] possible 'the measurement of overall phenomena, the description of groups, the characterization of collective facts, the calculation of the gaps between individuals, their distribution in a given population.'"[16]

Panoptic rationality, driven by the twin imperatives of productivity and efficiency, may be said to have reached its apotheosis in the late twentieth century; its sublime embodiment, the computer memory banks which support and reinforce an almost unimaginably vast documentary apparatus. Critics, among them Joseph Weizenbaum, maintain that the computer, far from transforming the social and political structure of Western society, has prolonged its ability to perpetuate itself, "by shoring up existing institutions and practices which might have collapsed under the sheer weight of increasing data."[17] The development of computer technologies has not only raised the ceiling on a recordkeeping system's capacity to store personal information; it has also greatly enhanced the benign surveillance power of the state and in the process created new possibilities for privacy invasion.

Perhaps the most fundamental aspect of the computer revolution involves changes in the form and nature of the information recorded. Information that was once recorded in conventional written or printed form is increasingly recorded in electronic form. Computer technology has contributed to the collection, preservation, and use of massive bodies of highly detailed information such as that describing individual characteristics, recording human transactions, or documenting the elements of social, economic, and political processes.[18] Information held in a variety of data banks can be processed and linked quickly, efficiently, and inexpensively. Computerized files can be quickly retrieved and easily and anonymously updated; they are readily accessible from many different points in an organization; and they can be easily merged, allowing a number of files dealing with the same individual to be compiled into a single dossier. Computerized files also can be easily transferred to another information user and combined with other files from other sources for other uses. This technological capability is alarming to privacy advocates because it facilitates "highly detailed analysis [which could] reveal relationships and permit the drawing of inferences of people not possible before the computer."[19]

Today, information about all major personal characteristics—vital statistics, social and geographic mobility, wealth, income, education, political affiliations—can be easily stored, organized, and disseminated in electronic form. One result of this, according to Arthur Schafer, has been that otherwise harmless (because scattered) data can be transformed into potentially harmful dossiers:

> Advanced technology has made extensive surveillance relatively easy and inexpensive. At the same time, the increasingly bureaucratic organization of social institutions (a feature shared by governments and multinational corporations) has made extensive surveillance and monitoring of individuals seem inevitable and desirable, at least to those whose power and other interests are enhanced by the result.[20]

The gathering of personal information by large organizations is a source of uneasiness because it renders citizens vulnerable to a technological voyeurism against which they are, largely, defenseless. Moreover, there is widespread concern that these organizations will use the information in ways that were not intended, or consented to, at the time of collection.[21] A major target of citizen concern has been the government, primarily because it is the largest information gathering organization in society.

In recent years, the widespread use of computer matching (or data matching and linkage) by government agencies has become a particular focus of privacy concern.[22] Computer matching refers to the computerized comparison of records for the purpose of establishing or verifying eligibility for a government benefit program or recouping payments or delinquent debts under such programs. Comparisons can be made by matching names, social insurance or social security numbers, addresses, or other personal identifiers. Computer matching has been used by government agencies to detect unreported income, unreported assets, duplicate benefits, incorrect personal identification numbers, overpayments, ineligible recipients, inappropriate entitlements to benefits, and service providers billing twice for the same activity.

Government agencies consider the purposes of computer matching, to detect fraud and track delinquent citizens, to be legitimate ones and defend the practice on the grounds of cost-effectiveness and efficiency. In the United States, the claim of cost-effectiveness has been disputed by the General Accounting Office, which in 1986 announced that government agencies lacked a reliable methodology for calculating costs and benefits of matching programs; and by the House Committee on Government Operations. In a report accompanying a 1988 bill to curtail computer matching, the House Committee stated flatly that, "the cost effectiveness of computer matching has yet to be clearly demonstrated." Given the demonstrably poor quality of data in several of the banks used for computer matching programs, these findings are hardly surprising. In many government agencies, audits of the quality of the records contained in various data banks are seldom, if ever, conducted.[23]

Even if cost-effectiveness and efficiency could be demonstrated, computer matching programs raise disturbing ethical questions to which reasons of economy offer an inadequate response. In *The Rise of the Computer State,* David Burnham questions the social priorities that underlie computer matching programs such as the nationwide parent locator system, established by the U.S. Congress, which tracks down runaway fathers to enforce child support payments that otherwise would have to be drawn from the federal Aid for Dependent Children program:

> First, did the narrowly focused congressional decision limiting its concern to cracking down on welfare cheats head off other more fundamental legal reforms that might have actually improved the stability of American families?
>
> Second, once a federally mandated tracking system is established that increases the power of county and state officials to trace the movements of one group of citizens, will the system inevitably come to be used for the surveillance of others who fall into disfavor?[24]

The danger of computer matching programs is that the bureaucratic and technological imperatives that drive them inevitably create possibilities for various forms of political and social control, possibilities that are difficult to resist. The suggestion that matching programs will only be used against fraudulent or delinquent citizens demonstrates a fundamental "error in perspective," according to Jacques Ellul, because the "rational and unblinking search for increased efficiency and greater productivity"[25] that underlies technology (or, to use Ellul's term, "technique"), means that "it tends to be applied anywhere it can be applied. It functions without discrimination because it exists without discrimination."[26]

Computer matching programs have also been criticized on the grounds that they violate a citizen's protection against unlawful search. Former Canadian Privacy Commissioner John Grace maintains that, "computer-matching turns the traditional presumption of innocence into a presumption of guilt . . . In matching, even where there is no indication of wrong-doing, individuals are subject to high technology search and seizure. Once the principle of matching is accepted, a social force of unyielding and pervasive magnitude is put in place."[27]

Computer matching programs demonstrate that much of the organizational interest in the private lives of individuals is generated by the desire to control deviant behavior through credit systems that attempt to minimize the number of poor credit risks and by "the [need] . . . to document and define . . . fine-grained bureaucratic obligations."[28] The enormous quantity of personal documentation required for medical insurance or welfare benefits, for example, serves mainly to establish eligibility for those services. Moreover, as James Rule points out in *The Politics of Privacy:*

> People . . . protest what they consider "unfair surveillance"—often in the same breath with which they demand more vigorous surveillance for purposes which they support. Nearly all people can point to some form of surveillance with which they are unhappy, either because they disapprove of the ends at which it is directed, or because it is inefficient in the pursuit of these ends. But most people remain quick to demand surveillance, whenever it seems to promise effective pursuit of ends which they deem desirable. Public and private bureaucracies are usually only too willing to accommodate these demands.[29]

Clearly, public demand for effective protection against tax evaders, suspected child abusers, illegal unemployment or workers' compensation recipients, welfare frauds, dangerous drivers, or doctors overbilling the medicare system, is partly responsible for the growth of surveillance.

There is no natural limit to the growth of surveillance and no area of an individual's life too private to attract bureaucratic surveillance. People disclose all manner of deeply sensitive information to medical personnel as one of the costs of modern medical care; they may reveal equally sensitive information to insurance companies when filing a claim.[30] As correlations are established between particular kinds of data, offering new possibilities for various kinds of social control, the demands for more personal data inevitably follow.[31]

Throughout history some measure of privacy has been traded for physical, social, and legal protection under the terms of the social contract underlying relations between citizens and government. This social contract is the philosophical basis of the state, and is defined by J. W. Gough as "a theory of political obligation, to explain the nature and limits of the duty of allegiance owed by subjects to the state, and of the right on the part of the state or its government to control the lives of its citizens."[32] Based on the fact that "every civilized community, perhaps any real community requires, in order that it may exist at all, a mutual recognition of rights on the part of its members, which is a tacit contract,"[33] social contract theory specifies the privileges and responsibilities foregone by citizens and placed in trust with the governing agency and the benefits citizens receive in return, for example, good government, protection from external threat, and a guarantee of selected individual rights, rights that can only be relinquished with the consent of the individual.

In the interest of the social contract, citizens are obliged to surrender a certain amount of their privacy. Nonetheless, the government's right to collect and store information about citizens is not an unlimited one. This right does not, for example, permit the government to disseminate personal information to third parties for unspecified purposes. The disclosure of personal information to third parties is contrary to the basic principle that individuals should be able to determine for themselves when, how, and to what extent information about them is communicated to others. Individuals have little control over whether or not their privacy is invaded by the government, since they are often denied benefits and services if personal information is not provided. For the government then to disseminate or permit others access to that information for use in unspecified ways is a serious threat to the right of individual privacy.

Over the last twenty years, the government's obligation to protect the information citizens disclose to it has been legally recognized. In response to public concerns over actual and potential administrative abuses of personal information by government agencies, most western countries have developed data protection laws which attempt to define and defend categories of private life as they relate to recordkeeping practices.[34] In *Obstacles to the Access, Use and Transfer of Information in Archives,* Michel Duchein outlines the main categories of information typically protected in data protection conventions and statutes. These include: civil status and filiation (births, marriages, divorces, deaths); health; wealth and income; penal and criminal proceedings; professional activity; political, philosophical, and religious opinions; and basic statistical documents.[35]

The principle underlying data protection legislation is that the personal information individuals must disclose to the government in connection with any of their transactions with the government should be held to a trust relationship and should create a duty of nondisclosure. The collection of personal information about private individuals by the government is, theoretically, prohibited where individuals do not have the right of access to that information, lack opportunity to rebut data that might be prejudicial, and have no opportunity to exercise control over its dissemination.

The U.S. Privacy Act of 1974[36] and the Canadian Privacy Act of 1983[37] have codified in similar ways a set of fair information principles designed to "minimize intrusiveness in the collection of personal information; maximize fairness in its use; and to provide reasonable and enforceable expectations of confidentiality."[38] Four principles are embodied in the American and Canadian legislation. The first principle asserts that agencies covered under the legislation shall not use or disclose personal information without the prior consent of the individual(s) to whom the information pertains.[39] Secondly, agencies must permit individuals to have access to personal information pertaining to them.[40] Individuals are entitled to request that information that they believe is not "accurate, relevant, timely or complete," be corrected; and if there is disagreement between an individual(s) and an agency as to the correct version of the facts contained in the record, the agency is required to note that disagreement in the record.

The third principle of fair information practices is found in the requirement of the two acts that agencies collect and maintain only such information as the agency needs to fulfill its operating requirements. In the U.S. Privacy Act, the information must be "relevant and necessary to accomplish a purpose of the agency;" in the Canadian statute, information is not to be collected "unless it relates directly to an operating program or activity of the institution." [41] Personal information should be collected as far as possible directly from the individuals to whom it relates, and individuals should be informed of the authority for collection, the agencies to which the information may be transmitted, and the routine uses to which the information may be put. Personal information that is used in administrative decision making also should be accurate, complete, and timely to assure fairness to individuals.[42] Finally, the existence of personal information banks maintained by federal agencies must be made public. Agencies are required to publish an annual index of their personal information banks, including in it details of the categories of individuals maintained in those banks, the type of information stored, and the practices of the agency regarding storage, retrievability, access, retention, and disposal.[43]

Although the American and Canadian laws apply to both manual and electronic recordkeeping systems maintained by federal agencies, the American law is more limited in scope than its Canadian counterpart. The scope of the U. S. Privacy act is determined by the phrase, "any record contained in a system of records." Within the meaning of the act, a *record* is:

> any item, collection, or grouping of information about an individual that is maintained by an agency, including,

but not limited to his education, financial transactions, medical history, and criminal or employment history and that contains his name, or the identifying number, symbol, or other identifying particular assigned to the individual, such as a finger or voice print or a photograph.[44]

But the record only falls within the scope of the act if it is maintained in a system of records, that is, "a group of any records under the control of any agency from which information is retrieved by the name of the individual or by some identifying number, symbol, or other identifying particular assigned to the individual."[45]

The requirement that records be retrievable by a personal identifier effectively excludes from the act's scope (hence protection), an enormous body of records containing personal information simply because they are not maintained in a filing system accessed by name, identifier, or assigned particular. For example, information about an individual contained in documents concerning an organization, which is filed only by the name of the organization, would be a record, but not in "a system of records." Computer technology enables even more personal records to be kept and retrieved outside a system of records. The requirement thus undermines the objective of the act to afford access to all records about an individual; the U.S. Privacy Protection Study Commission has identified examples of agencies altering recordkeeping practices to evade the act in this very manner.[46]

The reach of the Canadian Privacy Act is considerably broader. "Personal information," within the meaning of section three of the act, is "information about an identifiable individual that is recorded in any form including, without restricting the generality of the foregoing," nine specific types of personal information relating to the individual's race, national or ethnic origin, color, religion, age, or marital status, as well as information relating to the individual's education, medical, criminal, or employment history or information relating to financial transactions in which the individual has been involved;

identification numbers, fingerprints, personal opinions, and correspondence of a confidential nature are also included in the definition.[47] The act does not protect information about officers or employees of government agencies or government service contractors that relates to their positions or functions; nor does it protect personal information about individuals who have been dead more than 20 years.

There are no provisions for criminal penalties for the wrongful collection, use, or disclosure of personal information in the Canadian Privacy Act, which relies instead on Criminal Code sanctions against fraud, theft, or breach of trust.[48] Nor do Canadians have an established right to sue the federal government if they suffer some harm as a result of a breach of information privacy, since a privacy tort does not exist at the federal level.[49] In the U. S. Privacy Act, on the other hand, individuals can sue an agency for any damages incurred as a consequence of agency misconduct relating to the disclosure of personal information and criminal penalties may be levied at agencies or persons who willfully disclose personal information without authority.[50] However, injunctive relief is available only to force access to and amendment of records; and damages can only be awarded if it can be demonstrated that the plaintiff has suffered actual damage from an intentional agency action. As the Privacy Protection Study Commission has observed: "The vast number of systems involved, the need to establish willful or intentional behavior on the part of the agency, and the cost and time involved in bringing a lawsuit, often make enforcement by the individual impractical."[51]

Perhaps the most significant difference between the American and Canadian legislation is that the U. S. Privacy Act does not provide for an oversight agency (a Privacy Protection Commission), "that would, on a continuing basis, articulate privacy interests against competing forces."[52] The act is primarily self-enforcing, which means that, in most instances, individuals must take privacy complaints to court in order to defend their rights. The omission of an independent oversight agency is a critical impediment to the effective implementation of the act because, "quite simply, there is no vehicle for answering the question: 'Should a particular record-keeping policy, practice, or system exist at all?' "[53]

In the Canadian Privacy Act, such a vehicle does exist in the form of the Privacy Commissioner, who is authorized to audit compliance by government agencies with the provisions of the Privacy Act as well as investigate and make recommendations with regard to individuals' complaints about an agency's refusal to disclose, correct, or amend personal information. The act also gives the Commissioner extensive powers to investigate and report to Parliament on the general collection, retention, and disposal practices of government agencies.[54] At the Commissioner's discretion, investigations also may be periodically carried out on files contained in exempt banks.[55]

In creating the office of the Privacy Commissioner, the drafters of the legislation hoped that most privacy disputes could be resolved through mediation, without the need for recourse to the courts. The Privacy Commissioner's recommendations are not binding on an agency, though he is empowered to carry litigation on behalf of the requester if he believes the information should be made available to that individual over the objection of the government agency in question. He is not, however, empowered to bear the cost of litigation on behalf of individuals in the event an agency decides to disclose personal information without the individual's consent, "in the public interest." Agencies are only requested to notify the Privacy Commissioner before or at the time of disclosure.

The existence of an independent oversight mechanism for mediating privacy disputes between citizens and government agencies and questioning government recordkeeping practices is probably the Canadian Act's greatest strength. This does not mean that the mechanism has functioned as effectively as it might. Given the number of agencies covered under the Privacy Act and the consequent impossibility of the Commissioner's Office conducting comprehensive audits of more than a few government agencies, responsibility for auditing an agency's compliance with the act still rests primarily with the agency itself; a reality which does not inspire optimistic expectations for consistent compliance.[56] There is no mechanism for the Commissioner to challenge misuse of personal information (e.g., through computer matching programs) in the courts. Moreover, the Commissioner's consultative and advisory role has been undermined to some extent by the failure of government agencies to notify the Commissioner of proposed changes to administrative practices, statutes, draft legislation and regulations that have implications for personal privacy.[57]

The overall impact that privacy legislation has had on the relationship between citizens and recordkeeping agencies is difficult to determine. David Linowes and Colin Bennett, who have explored the implementation of the U.S. Privacy Act as a public policy issue, suggest that the reason for this stems from the fact that:

> policy goals are not defined in terms of achieving tangible results (such as distributing or redistributing a public good). The resource to be regulated is an elusive one. Violation of fair information practice is only visible in a tiny minority of circumstances. Hence, wrongful collection, storage, and dissemination of personal information (while in violation of the Privacy Act) may not expose actual harm to the individual concerned. There are no firmly established or measurable standards of evaluation.[58]

In its 1977 evaluation of the U. S. Privacy Act, the Privacy Protection Study Commission concluded that, while agency compliance with the act was difficult to assess because of the ambiguity of some of the act's requirements, compliance appeared to be "neither deplorable nor exemplary."[59] Much the same can be said about the Canadian act.

There is no doubt that the principles established in the American and Canadian Privacy Acts have had some effect on the way federal government agencies think about and treat personal information. The acts have exposed the nature and extent of recordkeeping systems in federal jurisdictions to a certain amount of public scrutiny; and they have travelled some distance in encouraging agencies to improve standard operating procedures for the collection, use, and dissemination of personal information. None of these changes can be considered insignificant.

Most critics of the American and Canadian legislation agree, however, that the effectiveness of both laws has been hobbled by vague statutory language, a less than comprehensive implementation framework, the lack of a public education mandate, and a continuing tendency on the part of many officials to exploit these weaknesses in a way that undermines the spirit of the legislation. Some of the barriers to the effective implementation of the acts have already been described. Other impediments include the open-ended interpretation of a "relevant and necessary" purpose taken by government agencies when applying the collection limitation requirement; the broad exemptions from the individual access requirement claimed by agencies;[60] and the exceptions—11 in the American law, 13 in the Canadian one—that hedge the individual consent requirement.[61]

The most controversial exception in both acts has been that permitting the use and disclosure of personal information for a "routine" or "consistent" use,[62] which is defined, ambiguously, as one compatible with the original purpose for which the information was collected. In both the United States and Canada, federal agencies have defined "compatible" broadly; computer matching, for example, is treated as a routine or consistent use of personal information, thereby exempting it from the consent requirement. The imaginative leap taken by agency officials in justifying computer matching on the grounds of routine use is illustrated by Linowes and Bennett in their account of a 1980 incident in which records maintained by the U.S. Office of Personnel Management (OPM) were released to the Veterans Administration (VA) to enable the VA to verify the accreditation of its hospital employees. According to Linowes and Bennett, "OPM claimed that the disclosure constituted a 'routine use' of its data because the agency believed 'that an integral part of the reason that these records are maintained is to protect the legitimate interests of government and, therefore, such a disclosure is compatible with the purposes for maintaining those records'."[63] In the drafting of the American and Canadian privacy legislation, the possibility of computer matching does not seem to have been anticipated, and its legality under both acts continues to be a matter of some debate.[64] John Grace's assertion that, "only an unacceptably broad interpretation of the words 'consistent use' could be used to justify computer matching as it is currently understood,"[65] reflects the position taken by most civil libertarians on this issue.

It is generally accepted that certain limitations on the right to information privacy are socially acceptable and even necessary. Data protection laws affirm the status of privacy as a *prima facie,* rather than an absolute, right because, in a democratic system, an individual's right to privacy must be balanced with rights stemming from society's commitment to other interests. From the perspective of the government, the right to individual privacy must be balanced against the state's prerogative in matters relating to law enforcement, program administration, national defense, and international relations, among other things. From the perspective of the citizens of the contemporary *polis,* the right against which the societal commitment to individual privacy must be balanced is that of freedom of information. The principle underlying freedom of information is that, generally speaking, every citizen should have the right to obtain access to government records to heighten the accountability of government and its agencies to the electorate; to enable interested citizens to contribute more effectively to debate on important questions of public policy; and to encourage fairness in administrative decision-making processes affecting individuals.[66]

Some critics charge that the legislative protection of information privacy is fundamentally incompatible with laws promoting freedom of information. Philosophically, the charge is erroneous because both privacy and freedom of information laws attempt to check government power by placing constraints on its control of information. However, at the level of statutory language, the competing values of disclosure and confidentiality are at times in conflict. When a citizen's right of access to government information is denied on the grounds that the exercise of that right will violate someone else's right to privacy, there is tension between a requester's rights under freedom of information law and an individual's rights under privacy law.

The tension between these two values becomes apparent when we look at the way the United States and Canada have attempted to balance, legislatively and judicially, the competing claims for access to information and the protection of personal privacy. The American and Canadian experiences offer contrasting case studies in their efforts to reconcile the values contained in each.

Notes

1. James Rule et al, *The Politics of Privacy: Planning for Personal Data Systems as Powerful Technologies* (New York: New American Library, 1980), 23.

2. Judith Rowe, "Privacy Legislation: Implications for Archives," *Archivists and Machine-Readable Records: Proceedings of the Conference on Archival Management of Machine-Readable Records, February 7-10, 1979, Ann Arbor, Michigan,* ed. Carolyn L. Geda, Erik W. Austin, and Francis X. Blouin, Jr. (Chicago: Society of American Archivists, 1980), 195.

3. *The Jerusalem Bible, Reader's Edition* (Garden City, N.Y.: Doubleday & Company, 1966), Genesis 3:21.

4. John Curtis Raines, *Attack on Privacy* (Valley Forge, Penna.: Judson Press, 1974), 23.

5. Hannah Arendt, *The Human Condition* (Chicago: University of Chicago Press, 1958), 24.

6. Roger Chartier, "Introduction," *Passions of the Renaissance,* vol. 3 of *A History of Private Life,* ed. Roger Chartier (Cambridge, Mass.: Harvard University Press, 1989), 15.

7. Michel Foucault, "On Governmentality," quoted in *The Foucault Reader,* ed. Paul Rabinow (New York: Pantheon Books, 1984), 14-15.
8. Ibid., 15.
9. Ibid.
10. Ibid., 16.
11. Ibid.
12. Ibid., 17.
13. Ibid.
14. Foucault, *Discipline and Punish: The Birth of the Prison,* trans. Ann Sheridan (New York: Vintage Books, 1979), 200.
15. Foucault, *Foucault Reader,* 20.
16. Ibid., 22.
17. See *The Myths of Information: Technology and Post-Industrial Culture,* ed. Kathleen Woodward (Madison, Wisc.: Coda Press, 1980), xvii.
18. Carolyn Geda, Erik W. Austin, and Francis X. Blouin, Jr., eds., *Archivists and Machine-Readable Records,* 8.
19. Jean Tener, "Accessibility and Archives," *Archivaria* 6 (Summer 1978): 28.
20. Arthur Schafer, "Privacy: A Philosophical Overview," (see chapt. 1, n.14), 2.
21. For a detailed examination of the threats to individual privacy presented by computer data banks, see, for example, Alan Westin, *Privacy and Freedom* (New York: Atheneum, 1967); Arthur Miller, *The Assault on Privacy: Computers, Data Banks, and Dossiers* (Ann Arbor, Mich.: University of Michigan Press, 1971); David Burnham, *The Rise of the Computer State* (New York: Random House, 1983); James Rule et al., *The Politics of Privacy* (New York: New American Library, 1980); Paul Sieghart, *Privacy and Computers* (London: Latimer New Dimensions, 1976); Malcolm Warner and Michael Stone, *The Data Bank Society: Organizations, Computers and Social Freedom* (London: George Allen and Unwin, 1970).
22. The use of computer matching by the U. S. government is documented in *Oversight of Computer Matching to Detect Fraud and Mismanagement in Government Programs,* Hearings before the Subcommittee on Oversight of Government Management of the Committee on Governmental Affairs, United States Senate, 97th Congress, 2nd Session, 15-16 December 1982 (Washington, D. C.: U. S. Government Printing Office, 1983), 1-2. In Canada, the results of a 1984 survey by the Treasury Board Secretariat on data matching were presented in hearings before the Standing Committee on Justice and

Solicitor General. See "Treasury Board Canada Report on Data Matching," Report presented in Hearings before the Standing Committee on Justice and Solicitor General on the Review of the Access to Information Act and Privacy Act, May 3, 1985.

23. Sociologist Kenneth Laudon, for example, found that slightly more than 50 percent of the records maintained in the FBI's computerized criminal history file were inaccurate or incomplete; the accuracy rate in three state systems studied ranged from 12 percent to 49 percent. See Kenneth C. Laudon, *Dossier Society: Value Choices in the Design of National Information Systems* (New York: Columbia University Press, 1986), 133-45. A study of the accuracy of juvenile records maintained by law enforcement procedures revealed similar findings. See U. S. Department of Justice, Bureau of Justice Statistics, *Juvenile Records and Recordkeeping Systems* (Washington, D. C.: Bureau of Justice Statistics, 1988).

24. David Burnham, *Rise of the Computer State*, 32.

25. Quoted in Burnham, *Rise of the Computer State*, 154.

26. Ibid.

27. Privacy Commissioner, *Annual Report: 1985-86* (Ottawa: Minister of Supply and Services, 1986), 7. See also the discussion of Project Match in the United States in Burnham, *Rise of the Computer State*, 208-11.

28. Rule, *Politics of Privacy*, 133.

29. Ibid., 135-36.

30. Ibid., 136. Various organizations in the United States and Canada collect and store information relating to an individual's sexual orientation on computer. The collection of such information is fueled by intolerance toward homosexuals and fear of AIDS. Among those collecting are medical organizations, insurance companies, investigative agencies, federal agencies, the military, and local health, police, and fire departments. See *Privacy Journal* 13 (10) (Sept. 1988); and Privacy Commissioner of Canada, *Aids and the Privacy Act* (Ottawa: Minister of Supply and Services, 1989).

31. Rule, *Politics of Privacy*, 136.

32. J. W. Gough, *The Social Contract*, 2nd ed. (Oxford: Clarendon Press, 1957), 244.

33. R. L. Nettleship, cited in Gough, *Social Contract*, 245.

34. Since 1974, most western countries, including Canada, the United States, the United Kingdom, France, Sweden, and the Federal Republic of Germany, have adopted data protection legislation. The Council of Europe and the Organization for Economic Co-operation and Development (OECD) have also

developed conventions that apply to electronic personal data files and electronic processing of personal data in the public and private sectors and require signatory states to give effect in domestic law to the basic principles of data protection embodied in the conventions. See Council of Europe, *Convention for the Protection of Individuals with Regard to Automatic Processing of Personal Data,* European Treaty Series No. 108, Strasbourg, 28 January 1981; and Organization for Economic Co-operation and Development, *Guidelines on the Protection of Privacy and Transborder Data Flows of Personal Data,* Paris: OECD, 1981.

35. Michel Duchein, *Obstacles to the Access, Use and Transfer of Information from Archives: A RAMP Study with Guidelines* (Paris: Unesco, 1983), 20-22.

36. 5 U.S.C., 552a.

37. *Privacy Act,* S.C. 1980-81-82-83, c.11, Section II.

38. [United States] Privacy Protection Study Commission, *Personal Privacy in an Information Society: The Report of the Privacy Protection Study Commission,* vol. 1 (Washington, D. C.: U. S. Government Printing Office, July 1977), 14-15.

39. 5 U.S.C., 552a(b); *Privacy Act,* S.C. 1980-81-82-83, c.111, 7.

40. 5 U.S.C., 552a(d); *Privacy Act,* S.C. 1980-81-82-83, c.111, 12.

41. 5 U.S.C., 552a(e) (1); *Privacy Act,* S.C. 1980-81-82-83, c.111, 4(1).

42. 5 U.S.C., 552a(e) (5); *Privacy Act,* S.C. 1980-81-82-83, c.111, 6(2). For judicial interpretation of the U. S. provision, see *Doe v. United States,* 781 F.2d 907 (D. C. Cir. 1986).

43. 5 U.S.C., 552a(e) (4); *Privacy Act,* S.C. 1980-81-82-83, c.111, 11.

44. 5 U.S.C., 552a(a) (4).

45. 5 U.S.C., 552a(a) (5).

46. See Privacy Protection Study Commission, *The Privacy Act of 1974: An Assessment,* Vol. 5: Appendix 4 to *The Report of the Privacy Protection Study Commission* (Washington, D. C.: U. S. Government Printing Office, 1977), 78, n.5. The one exception to the system of records requirement is contained in the act's prohibition on agencies maintaining records concerning an individual's exercise of First Amendment rights; the prohibition applies to such a record even if it is not incorporated into a "system of records." See 5 U.S.C., 552a(e) (7). See also *Clarkson v. IRS,* 678 F.2d 1368, 1374-77 (11th Cir. 1981); *Albright v. United States,* (I), 631 F.2d at 918-20.

47. *Privacy Act,* S.C. 1980-81-82-83, c.111, 3(a) to (i).

48. But see *R. v. Stewart,* October 26, 1988, 44 C.C.C. (3d) 109, 30 O.A.C. 169 (court ruled that confidential information cannot be stolen because it cannot be considered property for the purpose of the Criminal Code). A Revenue Canada employee who stole the income tax records of 16 million individuals from a Toronto office of Revenue Canada in 1986 was successfully prosecuted for breach of trust. However, the Privacy Commissioner points out that breach of trust would not apply "in situations where confidential personal information is taken by a nonpublic servant or is elicited by deceit from a public official." See Privacy Commissioner, *Annual Report: 1988-89* (Ottawa: Queen's Printer, 1987), 48-49.

49. See *Open and Shut: Enhancing the Right to Know and the Right to Privacy: The Report of the Standing Committee on Justice and Solicitor General Reviewing the Access to Information Act and the Privacy Act* (Ottawa: Queen's Printer, 1987), 48-49.

50. 5 U.S.C., 552a (i) (g).

51. Cited in David F. Linowes and Colin Bennett, "Privacy: Its Role in Federal Government Information Policy," *Library Trends* 35 (Summer 1986): 33.

52. David Flaherty, "Canadian Privacy Legislation in Comparative Perspective," *Conference on Privacy: Initiatives for 1984* (Toronto: Provincial Secretariat for Resources Development, 1984), 69.

53. Privacy Protection Study Commission, *Privacy Act of 1974,* 110.

54. *Privacy Act,* S.C. 1980-81-82-83, c.111, 37. The results of these investigations are documented in the annual reports of the Commissioner to Parliament as well as in special reports, such as the one examining the implications of the Privacy Act for the federal government's collection, use, and disclosure of AIDS related personal information. See Privacy Commissioner, *AIDS and the Privacy Act.*

55. *Privacy* Act, S.C. 1980-81-82-83, c.111, 36(1).

56. In his 1988-89 report, the Privacy Commissioner observed that some government agencies, notably the Canada Employment and Immigration Commission, had begun to conduct their own internal privacy audits. See Privacy Commissioner, *Annual Report: 1988-89,* 39, 47.

57. See *Open and Shut: Enhancing the Right to Know and the Right to Privacy,* 51-53.

58. Linowes and Bennett, "Privacy: Its Role in Federal Government Information Policy," 31.

59. Privacy Protection Study Commission, *Privacy Act of 1974,* 77.
60. For exemptions under the U. S. Privacy Act, see 5 U.S.C., 552a (j)-(k). For exemptions under the Canadian Privacy Act, see *Privacy Act,* S.C. 1980-81-82-83, c.111, 18-28.
61. See 5 U.S.C., 552a(b); *Privacy Act,* S.C. 1980-81-82-83, c.111, 7-8.
62. 5 U.S.C., 552a(b); *Privacy Act,* S.C. 1980-81-82-83, c.111(7)(a), (8) (2) (a).
63. Linowes and Bennett, "Privacy in Federal Government Information Policy," 32-33.
64. In both the United States and Canada, changes are afoot at the federal level to restrict government agencies' freedom to conduct computer matches. In 1988, President Reagan signed into law the Computer Matching and Privacy Protection Act, which prohibits federal agencies and state agencies using federal funds to suspend, terminate, reduce, or deny payments to an individual on the basis of a computer match without notifying the individual and permitting him or her an opportunity to challenge the "hit" in a hearing and appeal. See *Privacy Journal* 14 (10), (11) (August and October 1988): 1, 7.

In 1987, the Canadian government issued a policy paper outlining a new computer matching policy designed to ensure, among other things, that proposed data matches be approved, documented, and independently verified before being used in a decision-making process that directly affects an individual, and that an individual be given an opportunity to refute the information resulting from matches. See [Canada] Dept. of Justice, *Access and Privacy: The Steps Ahead* (Ottawa: Minister of Supply and Services, 1987).
65. Privacy Commissioner, *Annual Report: 1985-86,* 7.
66. John D. McCamus, "The Delicate Balance: Reconciling Privacy Protection with the Freedom of Information Principle," *Conference on Privacy: Initiatives for 1984* (Toronto: Provincial Secretariat for Resources Development, 1984), 51.

In Search of the Public Good

Balancing the Right to Privacy and the Right to Know

> Every human being has the right . . . to freedom in searching for truth . . . within the limits laid down by the moral order and the public good. And he has the right to be informed truthfully about public events.
>
> Pope John XXIII
> *Pacem in Terris*

Freedom-of-information laws are the legal embodiment of the public's "right to know" about its government. The right to know, like the right to privacy, is linked historically with the emergence of the principle of individual natural rights—Voltaire claimed, on behalf of natural freedom, the right of criticism and, therefore, of knowledge—and with the rebirth of the concept of democracy, according to which sovereignty derives from the people, who have the right to control the actions of the leaders they have chosen to govern them under the terms of the social contract.[1]

The acceptance of the people's right to rule, first articulated by Enlightenment thinkers and enshrined in both the French Declaration of the Rights of Man and of the Citizen and the American Bill of Rights, implied the state's obligation to make available the records of its own activities in the interest of keeping government visible and responsible. In *Democracy in America,* Alexis de Tocqueville defended the principle of the right to know on the grounds that, "when the right of every citizen to a share in the government of society is acknowledged, everyone must be presumed to be able to choose between the various opinions of his contemporaries and to appreciate the different facts from which inferences may be drawn."[2] The connection between the public's right to know and the right to information was made explicitly by James Madison, who maintained that "[a] people who mean to be their own governors, must arm themselves with the power knowledge gives. A popular government without popular information or the means of acquiring it, is but a prologue to a farce or a tragedy or perhaps both."[3]

The notion that citizens of a democracy must be given sufficient information about the workings of the government in order to make informed and intelligent decisions was enshrined in American law with the passage of the Freedom of Information Act (hereafter FOIA)[4] in 1966 (amended 1974) and in Canadian law with the passage of the Access to Information Act in 1983.[5] Both acts create a right of access to all government records that fall within the executive branch unless the records are exempt from access in order to protect other compelling interests, among them, the individual's interest in privacy.

Balancing the rights of the individual with the rights of the community as a whole presents an intractable problem to which legislative approaches usually offer less than ideal solutions. To ensure that the public's right to be informed about the conduct of government agencies and officials is not purchased at the cost of eroding individual rights to privacy and vice-versa, the public interest in disclosure must be weighed against the potential injury to the individual in each situation where the two rights collide. Legislators and courts in the United States and Canada have developed very different calculi for balancing the competing imperatives of public access and personal privacy, the effect of which has been to assert a bias for one value over the other. In the United States, the bias favors access; in Canada, privacy is given preference.

The U.S. FOIA preceded the U.S. Privacy Act by eight years and its reach is broader inasmuch as it permits access to records that are not maintained by the requester's identifiers and are therefore not "records" in "systems of records" within the meaning of the Privacy Act. In rare cases in which a record would be available under the Privacy Act, but exempt under the FOIA, the Privacy Act applies.[6] For many years following the implementation of the Privacy Act, court decisions were seriously split in dealing with cases where a record would be available under the FOIA but exempt under the Privacy Act; the Privacy Act contained no express provision for such a situation. Three Court of Appeals decisions held that a record exempt under the Privacy Act was not available under the FOIA.[7]

However, in 1982, in *Greentree v. U.S. Customs Service*,[8] the District of Columbia circuit explicitly rejected those decisions and ruled that the Privacy Act is not an exempting statute within the meaning of the FOIA's third exemption, which states that the act "does not apply to matters that are . . . specifically exempted from disclosure by statute." The *Greentree* view has since been endorsed by a number of other Circuit Court decisions,[9] and the Privacy Act amended in 1984 to read, "no agency shall rely on any exemption in this section to withhold from an individual any record which is otherwise accessible to such individual under the provisions of section 552 [the FOIA] of this title."[10] The issue now appears to be settled.

The FOIA treats individual privacy as a protectible interest. In accordance with exemption six of the FOIA, "personnel and medical files and similar files the disclosure of which would constitute a clearly unwarranted invasion of personal privacy" are exempt from the general rule of disclosure.[11] The purpose of the exemption, according to an early Senate report, is to balance the competing interests of individual privacy and freedom of information:

> The phrase "clearly unwarranted invasion of personal privacy" enunciates a policy that will involve a balancing of interests between the protection of an individual's private affairs from unnecessary public scrutiny, and the preservation of the public's right to government information. [12]

Where the balance is to be struck between the public interest in disclosure and the individual's right to privacy has emerged largely through case law.[13]

The accretion of judicial precedent has refined, to some extent, the interpretation of the notoriously vague criteria for a "clearly unwarranted invasion of privacy," established in exemption six. In *Department of the Air Force v. Rose*,[14] the Supreme Court determined that the phrase "the disclosure of which would constitute a clearly unwarranted invasion of privacy" modifies "personnel and medical files" as well as "similar files." The court maintained that Congress did not intend any *per se* exemption for personnel and medical files, but intended that their contents, like the contents of "similar files" be subject to the balancing process.[15]

Most courts have refused to focus on the nature or physical characteristics of the file in interpreting "similar files," preferring to move directly to an analysis of the privacy values implicated by the release. In *Rose*, for example, the Supreme Court held that case summaries of Air Force disciplinary actions were "similar files" because the disclosure of the summaries "implicates similar privacy values" as disclosure of personnel and medical files.[16] This interpretation was contradicted subsequently in *Washington Post Co. v. Department of State*,[17] which ruled that the exemption applies only to files containing information "of the same magnitude—as highly personal or intimate in nature—as that at stake in personnel and medical records." However, the Supreme Court reaffirmed the earlier interpretation when it reversed the *Washington Post* decision, maintaining that the phrase "similar files" is to have "a broad, rather than narrow meaning" and that it is the "balancing of private against public interests, not the nature of the files" that governs the applicability of the exemption.[18] The Supreme Court concluded that Congress intended exemption six to cover "detailed Government records on an individual which can be identified as applying to that individual" rather than simply "a narrow class of files containing only a discrete kind of personal information."[19] In light of the Supreme Court decision, agencies need only establish that the records in question apply to a particular individual to justify their designation as "similar files;"[20] the Courts of Appeals now routinely hold names and addresses to be "similar files."[21]

With respect to the meaning of "a clearly unwarranted invasion of privacy," court decisions have been uniform in holding that, in the language "clearly unwarranted," the statute "instructs the court to tilt the balance in favor of disclosure."[22] In *Rose,* the court declared that the privacy invasion must be tangible and substantial: "... Exemption 6 was directed at threats to privacy interests more palpable than mere possibilities."[23] Moreover, the court in *Arieff v. Department of the Navy* has held that it is the "production" of the records, not the resultant speculation to which they may give rise, by which the invasion of privacy must be measured.[24]

In the balancing process, a number of factors are analyzed by the court, including the existence and degree of the invasion of privacy, promises and expectations of confidentiality, the public interest in disclosure, and, somewhat controversially, the requester's interest in disclosure. With respect to the first factor, a substantial amount of case law has supported the view that material must usually be "personal" or "intimate" details of one's life;[25] and those cases that have protected records that are not obviously "intimate" personal details have usually involved little or no public interest in disclosure, as in *Wine Hobby USA, Inc. v. IRS,* [26] in which the names and addresses of amateur wine makers were protected from a commercial mailing; or reflect a fear of retaliation or harassment, usually in a labor-management context.[27]

An important principle established in the FOIA is that, in certain contexts, the conflict between freedom of information and the protection of individual privacy can be resolved by deleting the names of identifiable individuals before releasing the requested documents. The FOIA requires that, where the disclosure of an entire record would result in a clearly unwarranted invasion of privacy, "[a]ny reasonably segregable portion of [the] record shall be provided . . . after deletion of the portions which are exempt."[28] An agency, or District Court, must apply the exemption six balancing test with respect to each disputed portion of each document as its outcome differs from one portion to the next. In *Arieff* the court held that "the exemptions to the FOIA do not apply wholesale. An item of exempt information does not insulate from disclosure the entire file in which it is contained, or even the entire page on which it appears."[29] The possibility of segregating portions of records was a deciding factor for the Supreme Court in *Rose*; the case was resolved by the majority in favor of segregation and release.[30]

Courts have been reluctant to speculate in general terms about whether certain kinds of files are or are not exempt when determining the existence and degree of privacy invasion. In *Stern v. FBI,* for example, the court maintained that *"per se* rules of nondisclosure, based upon the type of document requested, the type of individual involved, or the type of activity inquired into, are generally disfavored."[31] Examples of records that have been found to be eligible for protection under exemption six, subject to removal of identifying details or a stronger interest in disclosure, include: case summaries of honor and ethics hearings maintained by the Air Force Academy;[32] names and addresses of Americans incarcerated in foreign prisons on drug charges;[33] the marital status of State Department employees;[34] prison records;[35] Department of Defense files detailing employment, personal histories, and religious affiliations;[36] the social security numbers of individuals in an Air Force investigative file;[37] property addresses, identities of lenders and loan amounts of Veterans Administration insured home loans;[38] and a Department of Agriculture study of housing containing information regarding marital status, legitimacy of children, medical condition, welfare payments, family fights, alcoholic consumption, and reputation, among other things.[39]

Examples of records that courts have found not to implicate privacy values or that implicate them only minimally include: most data in the Biographic Register of State Department employees (including date and place of birth, educational background, work experience, military service, promotion history, awards received);[40] the names and addresses of unsuccessful applicants for research grants from the National Center Institute;[41] institutional and personal names of researchers contracting with the CIA for drug research in the MK-ULTRA program;[42] statements of fellow employees to National Labor Relations Board (NLRB) investigators;[43] and lists of names and addresses of union members eligible to vote in a representational election.[44]

The public interest in disclosure is the core of the balancing test established in exemption six. The Supreme Court in *Rose* asserted that privacy must be balanced against "the preservation of the basic purpose of the Freedom of Information Act to open agency action to the light of public scrutiny;"[45] and, more specifically, "to permit the public to decide for itself whether government action is proper."[46] The weightiest cases for the public interest in disclosure are those in which the information will serve to inform the public about the conduct of agencies or officials. In *Rose,* case summaries of honors and ethics disciplinary proceedings were sought by a law review to assess the workings of a part of the military justice system, a purpose which the Supreme Court considered worthy. Other examples are *Arieff,* where the court found a strong public interest in the names, unit prices, quantities and dates of shipments of prescription drugs to the Attending Physician to Congress for prescription for congressional members, families, and staff;[47] *Ferri v. Bell,*[48] where the court found that an inmate's exposure of a deal between a prosecutor and a witness constituted an "indirect public purpose" that overcame the privacy interest in the witness's arrest record; *National Association of Atomic Veterans v. Dir., Defense Nuclear Agency,* where the disclosure of the names and addresses of servicemen who participated in an atmospheric nuclear weapons testing program was held to be in the public interest because the requester was a nonprofit veterans association seeking to conduct scientific and medical studies of adverse health effects of such testing, as well as to inform atomic veterans about Veterans Administration benefits[49] and; *Cochran v. United States,* where the court ruled in favor of disclosure of information relating to the misuse of public funds and facilities by a Major General of the Army.[50]

A public interest argument which rests upon the value of disclosure for oversight of government activity must be convincingly made. Courts have not viewed with favor "assertions of a public interest in merely 'monitoring' the operation of a federal program."[51] Disclosure is not likely to gain support from the courts if the requested information is not needed to inform the interested public, or if it would not further that objective even if released.[52] Courts also have been consistent in holding that the less disclosure is of interest to anyone but the requester, particularly if the interest is commercial, the less compelling is the public purpose of disclosure. The leading case is *Wine Hobby USA, Inc. v. IRS,* in which the court held exempt the names and addresses of amateur wine makers because the requester's purpose was purely commercial and "wholly unrelated to the purposes" behind the FOIA.[53] Similarly, union authorization cards have been held exempt in a number of court cases, at least partly on the grounds that only the employer stands to benefit from their disclosure.[54]

A subject of some controversy in FOIA debates concerning exemption six has been the relevance of the requester's interest in determining whether or not to disclose information. The debate was provoked initially by the decision in *Getman v. NLRB,*[55] in which law professors specializing in labor relations were allowed access to lists of names and addresses of employees eligible to vote in union representation elections in order to carry out research on certain policies of the NLRB relating to the certification process. The court concluded that the public interest would be well served by disclosure in this case because the plaintiffs' study might convince the NLRB to streamline its election supervision practices and rationalize the law in the area of election tactics.[56]

In its analysis of the public interest in disclosure, the court limited itself to considering only the plaintiffs' use of the lists; and it suggested that a restriction on any use other than the one proposed might be appropriate. Critics of the *Getman* decision argued that the FOIA's purpose is to provide for the disclosure of information to "any person," a provision which "prohibit[s] any drawing of distinctions between plaintiffs."[57] The court in *Getman* held that such a prohibition conflicts with the balancing requirement of exemption six, maintaining that the only way a court can consider both of the opposing interests under the privacy exemption is by focusing exclusively on the plaintiff's use of the information. For this test to work, the *Getman* court submitted, "a court's decision to grant disclosure under Exemption (6) carries with it an implicit limitation that the information, once disclosed, be used only by the requesting party and for the public interest purpose upon which the balancing was based."[58]

The long-term implications of the *Getman* decision remain to be seen. As critics of the decision point out, arguments for disclosure that focus on the legitimacy of a particular requester's use of the information rather than on the legitimacy of the disclosure itself could eventually undermine the public's right of access. The *Getman* court established that in interpreting exemption six, it is appropriate for the Court to define the parties entitled to receive files. In refuting this interpretation, Frank Rosenfeld argues that there is sufficient evidence in the Senate reports on the FOIA that, in establishing exemptions, Congress deliberately adopted a test whereby a file is released either to the public as a whole or not at all.[59] If the "need to know" criterion introduced by the Getman court were to become an acceptable means of resolving the conflict between privacy protection and freedom of information in difficult cases, the "any person" rule at the heart of the legislation would eventually be eroded. Since there is at least some privacy interest in most cases which are litigated, courts might be tempted to limit disclosure in almost every case.[60] The view that it is improper for a court to focus only on the particular requester's proposed use of the information was supported in *Robles v. Environmental Protection Agency*,[61] in which the court held that "disclosure was never to depend upon the interest or lack of interest of the party seeking disclosure;"[62] and in *Kurzon v. Department of Health and Human Services,*[63] the Court of Appeals argued that, "While we do not doubt that an array of legal scholars as impressive as that mustered in *Getman* is indicative of a substantial public interest, we do not believe that the capability of the individual requester is a proper subject of inquiry under exemption 6. . . . The purpose of the FOIA is to make information available to the general public."[64] Other cases, however, have been nearly unanimous in holding that the exemption six balancing approach is an exception to the act's general "any person" rule and that while the public interest is predominant on the disclosure side of the scale, the requester is part of the public, and his or her interest can be considered for that reason alone.[65] For similar reasons, the D.C. Circuit has suggested that limitations on the requester's use are inappropriate.[66]

The balancing of public and private interests in exemption six cases may be affected by special factors, among them: statutory policies on disclosure or confidentiality, which are usually given great weight by courts;[67] and common law concepts of privacy, in particular the concept of the "public figure" in defamation law, which has been used to support disclosure arguments.[68] Although sometimes relevant to the degree of invasion of personal privacy, a prior promise or expectation of confidentiality has not been considered determinative in exemption six cases. In *Ackerly v. Ley,* for example, the court held: "It will obviously not be enough for the agency to assert simply that it received the file under a pledge of confidentiality to the one who supplied it. Undertakings of that nature cannot, in and of themselves, override the Act."[69]

An individual's expectation of privacy can be weakened by an insufficiently complete promise of confidentiality[70] or by prior public disclosure.[71] On the other hand, court decisions have also determined that testimony to some personal facts is not a waiver of privacy for other such facts;[72] nor is the fact that information is on the public record somewhere in the country considered decisive in its effect on an individual's expectation of privacy.[73]

A fundamental incongruity that attaches to the application of exemption six is the absence of any provision permitting the individual to whom the information relates to have any say in the decision to disclose or withhold the information. Although exemption six was created to strike a balance between the individual's right to privacy and the public's right to know, critics argue that it "fails to take into consideration the possibility that individuals would not object to the release of information about them. Or, if they do object, it may not be against the release of all information." [74] And while the FOIA permits anyone who has been denied access to an agency's files to seek a court order compelling disclosure, it does not assure that notice will be given (either of the request or the judicial proceeding) to the individual to whom the information relates, whose interests are most clearly jeopardized by the request. In their discussion of the privacy exemption of the FOIA, Kimera Maxwell and Roger Reinsch maintain that if personal privacy were of genuine government concern, that interest could best be expressed by involving the individual in the decision to release such information, since he or she is most qualified to decide when an invasion of privacy is "clearly unwarranted." [75]

At the judicial level, FOIA case law has provided some useful interpretations of what the courts consider to be appropriate and inappropriate disclosures of personal information in the public interest. Nevertheless, the reliance on judicial interpretation of exemption six on a case by case basis has resulted in a high level of administrative uncertainty.[76] Agency officials who have the initial responsibility for responding to FOIA requests for personal information are frequently left with few guidelines with which to interpret the exemption. Such a lacuna invites inconsistency in decision making at best, and abuse at worst. The worst is revealed in the finding of Maxwell and Reinsch, in their 1985 study of the privacy exemption, that custodians in government agencies have used the exemption to protect agency privacy as much as individual privacy.[77] Individuals are, of course, free to pursue their request through the courts; in many cases, however, the financial costs involved limit this option to those individuals who can afford to exercise it.

Finally, there remains some doubt whether the balancing test established in exemption six weighs public and private interests in a truly equitable way. Although he acknowledges the difficulty of reconciling the competing interests, Arthur Miller worries that exemption six,

> perhaps unintentionally, has upset the prior balance between [privacy and access], apparently without taking sufficient account of privacy considerations. By establishing an across-the-board statutory policy directing disclosure of governmental records, the Act reverses the traditional presumption in favor of a citizen's personal privacy, and places the burden on the information-holding agency to find a specific statutory ground for refusing to honor a request for disclosure.[78]

There is little doubt that, at the level of statutory language, the words "clearly unwarranted" hedge the protection of the privacy interest.

If the FOIA's exemption six betrays a bias in favor of access, section nineteen of the Canadian Access to Information Act establishes a clear preference for the protection of privacy. Unlike the FOIA, which treats personal information as a protectible interest, indicating the harms or injury which unauthorized disclosure would occasion and then weighing the injury against the public interest in disclosure, the Canadian Access Act (which is a companion statute to the Canadian Privacy Act), treats personal information as a mandatory class exemption. Agencies are required to withhold the information, regardless of whether or not any injury to a private interest might result from its disclosure.

Under subsection 19(1) of the Access Act, an agency cannot disclose any record if it contains information that falls into one of the nine categories of personal information defined in section three of the Privacy Act. If a government agency refuses to disclose information requested under the act on the grounds that it constitutes personal information within the meaning of the Privacy Act, the individual seeking the information has the right to complain to the Information Commissioner (whose powers are analogous to those of the Privacy Commissioner), who will investigate the validity of the agency's refusal; but unless the information falls outside the protection of section three, the complainant does not, in most circumstances, have a supportable case. The Access Act's provision for judicial review of an agency's refusal to disclose personal information is similarly constrained. Though the act permits the Federal Court to order disclosure of personal information which, in the Court's opinion, falls outside the reach of section three, it does not give the Court latitude in determining whether substantial privacy values would be implicated by the disclosure of a record that falls within section three: the invasion is presumed.

The mandatory class exemption for personal information would seem to preclude any balancing of public and private interests. And yet, Canadian Professor of Law Murray Rankin has observed, though it purports to be mandatory, the provision, "is in fact a permissive exemption subject to a balancing test" [79] because it is qualified by various exceptions to the rule of nondisclosure which permit, albeit indirectly, a kind of balancing of interests. Under subsection 19(2), the head of a government institution may disclose personal information if the individual consents to disclosure;[80] the information is already publicly available or; disclosure of the information is permitted under a series of exceptions found in section eight of the Privacy Act.

The exception that addresses the balancing of public and private interests explicitly is subsection 8(2)(m)(i), which allows an agency to disclose personal information:

> ... for any purpose, where, in the opinion of the head of the institution,
> (i) the public interest in disclosure clearly outweighs any invasion of privacy that could result from the disclosure ...

The balancing of the public interest against the invasion of privacy in this provision is fundamentally different from FOIA exemption six cases. In Canada, the right to privacy is presumed and it is not necessary to demonstrate that there would be "a clearly unwarranted invasion of privacy" as in the United States. The words "clearly outweighs" "tip the balance in favor of privacy":

> Evidently, Parliament intended that, if having regard to all relevant circumstances, the public interest in disclosure evenly matches the resulting invasion of privacy, the information should not be disclosed. Therefore, the public interest in disclosure must be demonstrably greater to prevail over the privacy interest.[81]

Moreover, the provision does not imply a right of access to personal information by third parties. Instead, as the act's policy guide underlines, "the provision only permits disclosure by the institution where, in the discretion of the head of the institution, the appropriate conditions ... are met." [82] In deciding whether to disclose personal information under the provision, an agency must weigh the expectations of the individual, the sensitivity of the information involved, and the probability of injury to the individual in the event of disclosure, against the public interest in disclosure.

In the Canadian Act, promises and expectations of confidentiality weigh more heavily than they appear to in FOIA cases. The conditions governing the collection of the personal information and the expectations of the individual to whom it relates have been considered determinative in a number of cases. In one such case, Health and Welfare Canada refused to release a list of the respondents to an information letter proposing revised regulations for the control of food irradiation. The complainant argued that disclosure was in the public interest because, "where individuals and organizations make submissions to the government voluntarily for the purpose of influencing public decision-making and not pursuant to any statutory requirements of disclosure, the information should be made available to the public." [83]

The Commissioner found the complainant's claim insupportable. Critical to her finding was the fact that the department, in soliciting contributions, did not warn potential contributors that their names or information about them would be disclosed to the public. Since Health and Welfare Canada treated the names as confidential, the Commissioner accepted that this practice carried with it an implied promise of confidentiality. Moreover, she argued, even after the Access Act came into force, contributors may reasonably have relied upon the definition of personal information in section three of the Privacy Act, which includes "correspondence sent to a government institution by the individual that is implicitly or explicitly of a private or confidential nature." [84] On the other hand, if the information is unsolicited or given freely or voluntarily with little expectation of it being maintained in confidence; or if the individual has made a version of the information generally available to the public, the right to privacy may be considered waived.[85]

With respect to the degree of privacy invasion, the interim policy guidelines for the Access Act do not speculate on the kinds of information that are presumed to be either particularly sensitive or fairly innocuous. The guidelines do state that, in weighing the sensitivity of personal information, agencies may assume that privacy concerns diminish with the passage of time. They also suggest that agencies consider using the public interest provision when dealing with requests for personal information relating to deceased individuals who have been dead for less than 20 years (the Privacy Act protects personal information for 20 years after the death of the individual to whom the information relates); and they outline factors to be considered when making a decision whether to disclose such information.[86] Like the U. S. FOIA, the Canadian Access Act recognizes that conflicts between the two interests can be partially resolved through the severing of documents. The Access Act includes a provision requiring the disclosure of, "any part of ... [a] record that does not contain, and can reasonably be severed from any part that contains, any such information." [87]

Given the provision's general bias toward protecting personal privacy, it follows that the demonstration of harm required in the balancing process is less onerous than that envisaged in FOIA cases, where the harms resulting from disclosure must be "tangible and substantial" and "represent threats to privacy interests more palpable than mere possibilities." The guidelines define an injury as "any harm or embarrassment which will have direct negative effects on an individual's career, reputation, financial position, safety, health, or well-being." [88] In her interpretation of the injury criterion, the Information Commissioner has maintained that, "it is not necessary to show that specific harm will—or even may—be caused, but an invasion of privacy is obviously more serious if it does harm the one whose privacy has been invaded.... Such harm is difficult to predict, requiring examination of both the potential harm and the likelihood of harm." [89]

There is general agreement that the public interest concept "has no single, abstract definition. It may vary depending on the facts, on any express statutory purpose and on public or private attitudes." [90] Agency interpretations of what constitutes the public interest may be glimpsed in decisions to disclose, in accordance with this provision, information concerning a deceased Soviet scientist who had defected to Canada; information regarding Canadian government funding of the Allan Memorial Institute in the 1950s and 1960s; information on an inmate being released on parole; the blood type of an ex-armed forces member; the addresses of several inmates who were potential witnesses in a murder trial; and the seniority roll of RCMP officers (only after the removal of information relating to official language capacity, dates of retirement and years of continuous service).[91]

FOIA precedents have occasionally been invoked by complainants to support an argument for disclosure of personal information on the grounds of a public interest. The Information Commissioner has generally discounted the applicability of American FOIA precedents to Canadian cases because the balancing test in FOIA cases places a greater burden on the party objecting to the disclosure of personal information to prove why it should not be disclosed; in Canadian law, a greater burden is placed on the party seeking access to personal information to prove why it should be disclosed. She has refuted specifically the relevance of the decision in *Getman v. NLRB*: "The right of access under the Access to Information Act is to the public at large. Consequently, the particular use which a requester proposes to make of information and the limited extent to which he or she will disclose it further are not relevant to the right of access or the exemptions applied."[92]

Whether the public interest in disclosure is "demonstrably greater" than the privacy interest concerned will depend on a number of factors. In cases mediated thus far, it is clear the public interest must be compelling and constitute the only means through which that interest may be served. In a case involving an agency's refusal to disclose a list of applications for financial assistance to remove urea formaldehyde insulation from owners' homes, the Information Commissioner accepted that the purpose for which the complainant sought access—to demonstrate that potential home buyers could use the Access Act to ensure that they do not inadvertently purchase homes which might have been exposed to urea formaldehyde—was relevant to the public interest. However, "the compilation and release of the lists requested would result in disclosure of the names, addresses and financial data of already unfortunate individuals, contrary to the Privacy Act." [93] She concluded that a public interest in knowing whether a home has been exposed to urea formaldehyde occurs only when a home is put up for sale. In those circumstances, she argued, "the combined effect of the Privacy Act and the Access to Information Act . . . would allow real estate agents, mortgage lenders and lawyers to conduct a search with the consent of the vendor." [94]

The factors strengthening the argument for disclosure in the public interest vary, depending on the circumstances of a particular case. Examples of situations in which a public interest might outweigh the potential invasion of privacy are outlined in the interim policy guidelines. They include health or medical emergencies, accidents, natural disasters, or hostile or terrorist acts where the lives and well-being of one or more individuals depend on disclosure; when disclosure is needed to carry out an order of the court, for example, to enforce a custody order; and when disclosure of information relating to an individual is required either to substantiate a public statement made by the individual or to correct such a statement.[95]

A number of factors considered sufficiently compelling to support disclosure are summarized in *Mary Bland v. National Capital Commission*.[96] The case involves the refusal of the National Capital Commission (NCC) to disclose records containing the names of all the tenants of rental properties owned and administered by the NCC and the amounts of rent charged to each. The complainant maintained that she was seeking to confirm or refute persistent rumors that friends of the government received preferred treatment by being chosen as NCC tenants and by paying rents below market value. The Information Commissioner conducted an independent appraisal of the market value of some of the properties to determine if the allegations were substantive and solicited the views of current and former residential tenants on the matter. Her investigation revealed "a legitimate, overriding public interest" in disclosing the list requested because the leasing of NCC property "involves public money and public property and the public has a powerful interest in knowing how effectively and fairly the NCC deals with those who have financial dealings with the agency." [97] Although the tenants who responded to the Commissioner's solicitation argued strongly against disclosure on the grounds that the privacy invasion might subject them to harassment, the fact that the independent appraisal provided clear *prima facie* evidence that NCC rents were generally below market value proved to be an overriding factor in deciding for disclosure.

The NCC rejected the Commissioner's recommendation, maintaining that "the public interest in disclosure is less than apparent in this situation as there would be no general benefit for or advantage to the public to be provided with that information." [98] The case was appealed to the Federal Court, which concurred with the Commissioner's recommendation. In its judgment, the court chastised the NCC for failing to evince any weighing of the factor of invasion of privacy against that of the public interest in disclosure: "The 'public interest in disclosure' is a statutory Polaris, and it is not to be cursorily denigrated by the simple assertions that it is 'less than apparent in this situation' and that 'there would be no general benefit for or advantage to the public to be provided with that information.' Such assertions do not constitute any weighing of one statutory factor against the other." [99] The court determined, on the evidence of the Commissioner's findings, that the public interest clearly outweighed any invasion of privacy and ordered the disclosure of the information.

Apart from the explicit balancing test of the public interest provision, section eight of the Privacy Act contains a number of other provisions designed to balance private and public interests. Research interests in particular are addressed in subsection 8(2)(j), which permits access to personal information for research and statistical purposes under specified conditions; 8(2)(k), which allows access to individuals researching or validating native land claims; and section 8(3), which allows personal information in the custody of the National Archives of Canada to be disclosed in accordance with section six of the Privacy Regulations.[100] The section permits the National Archives to disclose personal information if "the information is of such a nature that disclosure would not constitute an unwarranted invasion of privacy." [101] The provision was designed specifically to permit research access to personal information in the custody of the National Archives of Canada under conditions less onerous than those established either under the general research provision or the public interest provision. Records containing personal information are subjected to a balancing test very similar to that provided under exemption six of the FOIA; the resemblance to the FOIA exemption is underlined in the National Archives' *Guidelines for the Disclosure of Personal Information for Historical Research,* which interprets an invasion of privacy as "a situation in which the disclosure of personal information would clearly result in harm or injury to the individual to whom it pertains." [102] The provision is distinct from exemption six, however, inasmuch as it confers on the National Archives a discretion to disclose; it does not create a right of access to such information.

In determining the existence and extent of the invasion of privacy, factors similar to those established under the public interest provision are taken into account, including, the expectations of the individual(s) to whom the information pertains, the sensitivity of the information relative to its contents and currency, the probability of injury (injury being defined as any harm or embarrassment which will have direct negative effects on an individual's career, reputation, financial position, health, or well-being), and the context of the file.[103] For the purposes of the invasion of privacy test, certain types of personal information—medical, criminal and law enforcement, and financial—are presumed to be more sensitive than other types of personal information.

Finally, the balancing of public and private interests is implicit in the Privacy Act's exclusion of eight categories of personal information from the protection of section three. These include information about officers or employees of a government institution that relates to their positions and functions (e.g., title, classification, salary range, responsibilities, personal opinions or views given in the course of employment) (3(j)); information about government service contractors relating to the service performed, including the terms of the contract, the name of the individual concerned, and the opinions or views of that individual in the course of the performance of such services (3(k)); information relating to any discretionary benefit of a financial nature, including the granting of a license or permit (3(l));[104] and information about an individual who has been dead more than 20 years (3(m)).

Much of the criticism of the Canadian approach to balancing public and private interests has focused on the way in which "it resolves the conflict between access and privacy by simply suppressing it into the level of administrative discretion." [105] Under subsection 19(2) of the Access Act, access to records containing personal information is denied as a matter of right; instead a discretion to disclose such information is conferred on public officials. This discretionary power is bound to create inequities in access. When the disclosure of personal information may expose a government agency or its officials to public criticism or embarrassment, the head of the agency is clearly in a conflict of interest in determining whether or not to release such information. Under these circumstances, "the shield of privacy [may be] held up to protect abuses ... that are in no manner personal." [106] On the other hand, government officials may also use their discretion to disclose information that is clearly invasive of individual privacy to further an agency's interests.

In the one judicial decision relating to the interpretation of a government official's discretion to withhold or disclose personal information under the federal act, there is evidence that such a discretion was intended to be limited. In *Information Commissioner v. Minister of Employment and Immigration,*[107] the Federal Court rejected the agency's argument that subsection 19(2) of the Access Act creates the possibility of access in "a wholly discretionary setting." In rendering its decision, the Court concluded that, as a matter of statutory interpretation, and to be consistent with the basic purpose of the act, subsection

19(2) establishes a discretion to release personal information under certain circumstances. It maintained further that, "those conditions having been fulfilled, it becomes tantamount to an obligation upon the head of the government institution to do so, especially where the purpose of the statute was enacted is, as here, to create a right of access in the public."

The explicit privacy bias in the Canadian law has also come under attack. The Canadian Historical Association and the Social Science Federation of Canada, for example, believe that the purposes of the Access Act would be better served if the bias of the public interest provision were reversed to favor access rather than privacy, as the FOIA's exemption six does.[108] Unquestionably, the Access Act approaches the public interest in an unnecessarily circuitous fashion, and the language in which the public interest provision is couched discourages government officials from weighing the competing interests of access and privacy equitably. The inadequacies of the Access Act are not, however, likely to be corrected through the adoption of the FOIA model. There are two reasons why this is so. First, as we have already seen, the vague standard of exemption six is likely, at the government agency level, only to increase the discretion of government officials to interpret public and private interests to their own advantage. Second, although a reversal of the Canadian bias toward privacy might alleviate one set of problems, it might, equally, create a standard for disclosure that may prove insupportable in the long term.

In arguing for the public interest, as against a private interest, it is important to be very precise about what we are defending. The concept of the public interest has been greatly taxed in recent years, to the point where it is in danger of collapsing beneath the weight of the claims made on its behalf. While it is true that government agencies are prone to cloaking government secrecy in the guise of personal privacy, it is equally true that particular constituencies within the general public occasionally are guilty of appropriating the public interest and recreating it in their own image. The concept of the public interest can be stretched to a point where it disappears into abstraction, as when contemporary historians, for example, maintain that "a case can be made for letting historians see the complete record, whatever its implications, on the philosophical grounds that a thorough study of history can preserve national humility and reduce the repetition of stupidities." [109]

In defining the public interest, it is necessary to winnow out from myriad diverse interests what is common, shared, and essential. Historically and philosophically, the public's right to know, on which the public interest is commonly defended, is justified in terms of the requirements of citizenship and political action. The community's welfare provides grounds for the protection of the right to know; the public at large should have access to the information it needs to vote and conduct its affairs intelligently. "Vindicating the 'people's right to know'," Peter Bathory and Wilson McWilliams argue, "does not require that all specialized, private, and relatively inaccessible information be 'made public.' It demands, rather, that the public have access to those facts necessary for public judgment about public things." [110]

Moreover, the public interest may, at times, be better served by secrecy than by openness. Arthur Miller suggests that,

> One very important public interest to be weighed is the protection of individual privacy and the preservation of citizen faith in the government's discreet use of personal information. The release of sensitive personal information by public officials may engender distrust of the government and inhibit its efforts to obtain the information needed to govern effectively.[111]

Arguments for disclosure on the grounds of the public interest frequently fail to acknowledge the "competing dimensions of the public interest." In *A Matter of Principle,* Ronald Dworkin points out that, although the U.S. FOIA has resulted in the disclosure of much valuable information,

> ... pressure has been building for substantial amendment. Doctors point out that double-blind experiments testing new drugs and procedures are ruined when reporters discover information that destroys the confidentiality that makes the experiments statistically significant. Scientists argue that the incentive to carry on research may be jeopardized when newspapers publish details of interesting grant applications.[112]

It is "bizarre," Dworkin suggests, to assert that, even if the public, acting through its legislators, wishes to amend the FOIA to exempt preliminary reports of medical research because it believes that the integrity of such research is more important than the information it provides, it ought not to do so because of its own right to have that information.[113] Similarly, the public interest in preserving the liberties promoted by privacy, for example, freedom of association, the right to due process, or the right to be protected against self-incrimination, may, at times, override society's interest in information.

Limitations on public disclosure also can be justified if they are essential for the protection of certain confidential relationships that exist between citizens and the government. In such cases, a balancing of public and private interests may be inappropriate, as the Ontario Commission on Freedom of Information and Individual Privacy Act makes clear:

> If [a legislative body] concludes that trade union member certification votes or interview notes relating to children involved in custody disputes should be granted absolute confidentiality, specific statutory provisions rendering such information confidential may be a much more desirable means of reconciling the publicity/confidentiality tension than the delegation of the matter to an adjudicator who would apply a (necessarily somewhat vague) balancing test.[114]

Given the societal interests they protect, many statutory confidentiality provisions are not an unreasonable constraint on the public interest. Nevertheless, as the recent findings of the Canadian Standing Committee on Justice and Solicitor General suggest, statutory prohibitions against disclosure are frequently drafted more broadly than is needed to protect privacy interests and thus should be assessed on a case-by-case basis.[115]

A thoughtful approach to the problem of balancing private and public interests is taken in the Ontario Freedom of Information and Protection of Privacy Act of 1987.[116] After examining the U.S. FOIA and the Canadian Access to Information Act, the Ontario Commission on Freedom of Information and Individual Privacy concluded that a more equitable balancing test than that provided for in the Canadian Act should be embodied in Ontario's privacy exemption; but that such a balancing test should provide clearer guidance than is afforded by the "clearly unwarranted invasion of privacy" test in the FOIA.

The Ontario Commission identified three requirements that the privacy exemption should meet.

- The statute should, to the greatest extent possible, identify clearly situations in which there is an undeniably compelling interest in access;

- For those cases not resolved by such explicit provisions, a general balancing test should be stated with some indication of the factors to be weighed in an application of the test to a particular document;

- As part of the criteria set forth for the application of the balancing test, personal information which is generally regarded as particularly sensitive should be identified in the statute and made the subject of a presumption of confidentiality.[117]

Rather than characterize the nature of the information that should, under normal circumstances, be protected from disclosure, as is done in the FOIA's exemption of "personnel and medical files and similar files," the privacy exemption in the Ontario Act, like its federal counterpart, identifies specific categories of personal information[118] that are normally protected from disclosure.

Under the Ontario Act, the situations justifying the disclosure of personal information in the public interest include when the individual to whom the information relates has either requested or consented to disclosure; when access to personal information is necessary in order to respond adequately to an emergency situation involving serious risk to the health or safety of an individual; when the personal information was collected and maintained specifically for the purpose of creating a record available to the general public; when disclosure is expressly authorized under a provincial or federal statute; for research purposes under specified conditions; or, when the disclosure does not constitute "an unjustified invasion of personal privacy." The language of this last provision more equitably balances the interests at stake than does either the "clearly unwarranted invasion of privacy" criterion of the FOIA's exemption six or the public interest provision in the Canadian Privacy Act.

In determining whether a disclosure of personal information constitutes "an unjustified invasion of privacy," a number of relevant circumstances, similar to those established in exemption six court cases, are considered. Under the Ontario Act, disclosure is favored if it is desirable for the purpose of subjecting the activities of the government and its agencies to public scrutiny; if it will promote public health and safety; or, if it will promote informed choice in the purchase of goods and services. Disclosure is also favored if the personal information is relevant to a fair determination of rights affecting the person who made the request.

Disclosure is discouraged if it will expose the individual to whom the information relates to pecuniary or other harm; if disclosure is a likely impediment to a fair hearing; if the personal information is highly sensitive; if the information is unlikely to be accurate or reliable (the circumstances under which the information was gathered or submitted, and agency verification procedures will provide clues about the accuracy or reliability of the information); if the disclosure may unfairly damage the reputation of any person referred to in the record; or, if the personal information has been supplied by the individual to whom the information relates in confidence.

Finally, under the Ontario Act, a disclosure of personal information is presumed to constitute an unjustified invasion of privacy where the personal information:[119]

(a) relates to a medical, psychiatric or psychological history, diagnosis, condition, treatment or evaluation;

(b) was compiled and is identifiable as part of an investigation into a possible violation of criminal law, except to the extent that disclosure is necessary to prosecute the violation or to continue the investigation;

(c) relates to eligibility for social service or welfare benefits or to the determination of benefit levels;

(d) relates to employment or educational history;

(e) was obtained on an income tax return or gathered by an agency for the purpose of collecting a tax;

(f) describes an individual's finances, income, assets, liabilities, net worth, bank balances, financial history or activities, or creditworthiness;

(g) consists of personal recommendations or evaluations, character references or personnel evaluations; or

(h) indicates racial or ethnic origin or religious or political beliefs and associations.

Disclosure, in these cases, is justifiable only when the public interest it will serve is undeniably compelling.

The privacy exemption in the Ontario Freedom of Information and Protection of Privacy Act is considered by many to be a more useful legislative model for balancing access and privacy rights than either the U.S. FOIA or the Canadian Access to Information Act. In many respects, this assessment is valid. By identifying situations in which there is a strong public interest in access, indicating the factors to be weighed in balancing public and private interests in more ambiguous situations, and making particularly sensitive kinds of personal information subject to a presumption of confidentiality, the drafters of the Ontario Act have succeeded in defining in a more concrete way the nature of, and limitations on, public and private interests affecting the disclosure of personal information.

A striking feature of the Ontario Act, and one that deserves further exploration, is its explicit identification of research interests as a compelling public interest justifying the disclosure of personal information. By establishing research access (under specified conditions) as a freedom of information right, the Ontario Act draws a kind of equivalence between the public interest and society's need for knowledge. Freedom of inquiry in the pursuit of knowledge is a value in its own right. But is it equivalent to, or sufficiently analogous to, the public right to know as we have come to understand that term?

In the use of personal information for research and statistical purposes, the tension between the competing objectives of access and privacy protection is most palpably realized. Few would dispute that a wide range of societal benefits derive from research; nor would many question that granting the research community access to government-held personal information, relevant to legitimate research objectives, serves significant societal interests. Medical records, although they contain some of the most sensitive personal information, provide some of the most valuable raw data for medical and epidemiological research. One of the most contentious issues in data protection debates is data linkage; yet it is viewed by the research community as an enormously powerful means of correlating different factors that may influence particular phenomena. The linkage of employment records and mortality data, for example, increases greatly the significance of research results in the area of occupational health and safety.[120]

Government records have always been a significant source for the study of a wide range of social phenomena, such as affluence, poverty, authority, obedience, deviance, and mortality. In the late nineteenth century, Emile Durkheim relied on published summaries of statistical data to illuminate the causes of suicide. In the last half of the twentieth century, technological advances in government recordkeeping systems and the expansion of regulatory and social welfare programs have increased dramatically the research potential of government-held personal information. Government data files represent a major source of documentation for a wide range of research purposes, containing as they do demographic information, such as age, sex, marital status, and place of residence; socio-economic information, such as occupation, education, and income; and attitudes and opinions.[121] Data files can be linked with one another, creating a wealth of material for scientific and social research. Common attributes such as geographic location, occupation, age, and sex permit the linkage of a file with groups possessing similar attributes. Personal identifiers such as name and social security number permit even more sophisticated data linkage.

Defenders of research and statistical uses of personal information take the position "that existing personal data should be used as much as possible to promote scientific understanding of contemporary problems;" [122] they argue, further, that the legal and ethical problems associated with providing access to personal information would be simplified if a clear distinction were made between administrative and research uses of such information. David Flaherty defines research and statistical uses of personal information as, "uses which do not directly affect a particular person on the basis of the specific data in question. These are in sharp contrast to administrative or regulatory uses of data which directly affect a person in one way or another."[123] In most studies researchers are interested in the individual primarily as a carrier of attributes or characteristics of groups or distributions. Although individual data are often used as major building blocks during the analytical process, in the final stage, both research findings and statistical data are presented in aggregate form.[124]

The development of data protection legislation has become a matter of some concern to the research community because of the constraints such legislation places on research. Current legal standards governing the protection of personal information held in government agencies frequently fail to take into account the desirability of permitting research access to personal information: in many jurisdictions, statutes regulating certain categories of sensitive personal information, for example, health-related data, or criminal justice data, lack provisions allowing access for legitimate research purposes. Under both the Canadian and American Privacy Acts, access to government-held personal information for research and statistical purposes is left to the discretion of individual government agencies. Moreover, under the U.S. legislation, access to personal records within a system of records is permissible only if the records are transferred in a form that is not individually identifiable.

Researchers argue that placing prohibitions on research into areas that might invade individual privacy will severely hamper research and make certain studies impossible to conduct. Some researchers even maintain that the concept of invasion of privacy is irrelevant to statistical studies because data are not released in individually identifiable form. The statistical treatment of data already available (for example, information contained in administrative records), they suggest, should be permitted so long as confidentiality can be assured, since this does not constitute invasion of privacy.[125]

In 1977, in response to wide-spread concerns over the chilling effect prohibitive data protection laws might exercise over research, representatives from the research communities of five countries met in Bellagio, Italy, to discuss ways of improving access to government records, particularly statistical records. The participants reached a consensus on a number of key points, among them: that there are valid and socially significant fields of research for which access to microdata is indispensable; that there are legitimate research uses which require the utilization of identifiable data within a framework of concern for confidentiality; and that some research and statistical activities require the linking of individual data for research and statistical purposes. [126]

Acknowledging the importance of research and statistical uses of personal information, however, does not dispel the ethical ambiguities associated with such uses. The disclosure of personal information without the consent of the individual concerned runs counter to the principle that individuals should be able to exercise some control over the way government agencies use information relating to them. Another concern is that the disclosure of certain kinds of sensitive personal information—the obvious example is medical information—compromises the integrity of socially recognized confidential relationships. Finally, even if data linkage is directed at research, rather than administrative goals, it nevertheless conjures the worrying specter of new and potentially damaging dossiers.

These ambiguities are exacerbated by the fact that existing law and practice do not recognize a distinction between research and administrative uses of personal information and, in most cases, do not extend statutory protection to research records. As a consequence, individuals do not have any protection from inadvertent exposure to an administrative action as a consequence of supplying information indirectly for a research or statistical purpose when, for example, they apply for benefits under an agency program that uses client information for such purposes.

Ethical dilemmas notwithstanding, the research community is becoming a more active consumer of administratively produced personal information and is beginning to rely increasingly on the custodians of government records to make such information available for research. The Ontario Freedom of Information and Protection of Privacy Act provides for the disclosure of personal information for a research purpose if "the disclosure is consistent with the conditions or reasonable expectations of disclosure under which the personal information was provided, collected or obtained." The U.S. Privacy Protection Study Commission has recommended that the U.S. Privacy Act be amended to include a similarly worded provision.[127] The question is, how narrowly or broadly should such a provision be interpreted?

It is possible to argue that research directed at evaluating a government program constitutes a consistent use of the personal information collected under that program because such use serves government accountability. Medical and epidemiological research can rarely be considered a consistent use of government-held personal information unless the information was originally collected for such purposes. Nevertheless, the tangible benefits of such research are usually considered to constitute an indirect public interest sufficiently compelling to justify disclosure.

Appeals to government agencies to improve on provisions allowing research access to personal information, however, have not come solely from researchers engaged in epidemiological, evaluation or treatment research. Over the last twenty years, the focus of much historical research on the so-called "nonelites" of society, has also created a demand for a greater variety and quantity of records containing personal information; and, as Margaret Hedstrom notes, "the focus of historical research on the composition, attitudes and behavior of nonelites is precisely the same population on which government agencies compile and maintain extensive documentation." [128] In many cases, records containing personal information are sought by historians, not so much for their evidential value as government records but for their informational value. Added to the historical studies of various government agencies—analyses of programs, services, and client populations—are research projects that seek to document the lives of ordinary people with no particular emphasis on their status as clients of government agencies.[129]

From the perspective of government archivists, into whose custody a great deal of the kinds of personal information being sought is eventually delivered, it is likely this constituency of researcher that will place the greatest demands on the administration of access to personal information that has been transferred to government archives. In responding to requests for records containing personal information, archivists will be forced, increasingly, to grapple with difficult questions about the appropriate balance that should be struck between society's need for knowledge and the individual's need to be private. The trends in historical research that have precipitated increased demands for access to personal information held in government archives and the effect of these demands on the archival administration of access will be the subject of the next chapter.

Notes

1. Duchein, *Obstacles to Access, Use and Transfer of Information* (see chapt. 2, n.35), 3.
2. Alexis de Tocqueville, *Democracy in America*, vol. 1. (New York: Vintage Books, 1945), 190.
3. Quoted in Frank A. Rosenfeld, "The Freedom of Information Act's Privacy Exemption and the Privacy Act of 1974," *Harvard Civil Rights—Civil Liberties Law Review* 11 (1976): 607.
4. 5 U.S.C., 552.
5. *Access to Information Act*, S.C. 1980-81-82-83, c.111, Section I.
6. 5 U.S.C., 552a (q) (1).
7. See *Shapiro v. DEA*, 721 F.2d 215 (7th Cir. 1983), *cert. granted*, 466 U.S. 926 (1984); *Painter v. FBI*, 615 F.2d 689 (5th Cir. 1980); *Terkel v. Kelly*, 599 F.2d 214 (7th Cir. 1979), *cert. denied*, 444 U.S. 1013 (1980).
8. *Greentree v. U. S. Customs Service*, 674 F.2d 74 (1982).
9. See *Porter v. U. S. Department of Justice*, 717 F.2d 787 (3d. Cir. 1983); *Provenzano v. Department of Justice*, 722 F.2d 36 (3d. Cir. 1983), *cert. granted*, 466 U. S. 926 (1984) (No. 83-1045); *Clarkson v. IRS*, 678 F.2d 1368 (11th Cir. 1981) at 1376 (*dictum*).
10. 5 U.S.C., 552a (q) (2).
11. 5 U.S.C., 552 (b) (6).

12. S. Rep. No. 813, 89th Cong., 1st Sess. (1965) at 9. See also H. R. Rep. No. 1497, 89th Cong., 2d Sess. (1966) at 11.

13. The FOIA court cases cited in this chapter are taken from Allan Adler, ed., *Litigation under the Federal Freedom of Information and Privacy Act,* 14th ed. (Washington, D. C.: American Civil Liberties Union Foundation, 1989).

14. *Department of the Air Force v. Rose,* 425 U. S. 352.

15. *Rose,* 425 U. S. at 370. See also *Arieff v. Department of the Navy,* 712 F.2d 1462 (D. C. Cir. 1983).

16. *Rose,* 425 U. S. at 376-77. See also *Harbolt v. Department of State,* 616 F.2d 772, 774 (5th Cir. 1980).

17. *Washington Post v. Department of State,* 647 F.2d 197, 198-99 (D. C. Cir. 1981), *rev'd* 456 U. S. 595 (1982), quoting from *Simpson v. Vance,* 648 F.2d 10, 13 (D. C. Cir. 1980) in turn quoting from *Board of Trade v. Commodity Futures Trading Commission,* 627 F.2d 392 (D. C. Cir. 1980) at 398. See also *Sims v. CIA,* 642 F.2d 562, 573 (D. C. Cir. 1980).

18. *Department of State v. Washington Post Co.,* 456 U. S. 595 (1982) at 600.

19. *Department of State,* 456 U. S. at 602.

20. See *Hemenway v. Hughes,* 601 F. Supp. 1002, 1005 (D.D.C. 1985).

21. See *Minnis v. U. S. Department of Agriculture,* 737 F.2d 784, 786 (9th Cir. 1984); *VanBourg, Allen, Weinberg & Boger v. NLRB,* 728 F.2d 1270, 1272 (9th Cir. 1984).

22. *Getman v. NLRB,* 450 F.2d 670, 674 (D. C. Cir. 1971). See also *Rose,* 425 U. S. at 378 n.16 (phrase is "the major restraining feature" of exemption 6 which controls the ability of the agency to withhold information).

23. *Rose,* 425 U. S. at 380 n.19. See also *Washington Post Co. v. Department of HHS,* 690 F.2d 252, 261 (D. C. Cir. 1982) ("... under exemption 6, the presumption in favor of disclosure is as strong as can be found anywhere in the Act"). See also *Arieff,* 712 F.2d at 1467 (requests for the names, unit prices, quantities, and dates of shipments of prescription drugs to the Attending Physician to Congress for prescription for congressional members, families, and staff was held to pose only the "mere possibility" that particular diseases could be linked to particular patients).

24. *Arieff,* 712 F.2d at 1469.

25. See, for example, *Rose,* 425 U. S. 352 (1976); *Rural Housing Alliance v. Department of Agriculture,* 502 F.2d 1179 (D. C. Cir. 1974).

26. *Wine Hobby U.S.A. v. I.R.S.,* 502 F.2d 133, 135 (3d Cir. 1974).
27. See, for example, *Howard Johnson Co. v. NLRB,* 618 F.2d 1 (6th Cir. 1980); *Madiera Nursing Center Inc. v. NLRB,* 615 F.2d 728 (6th Cir. 1980); *Pacific Molasses Co. v. NLRB,* 577 F.2d 1172 (5th Cir. 1978); *Committee on Masonic Homes v. NLRB,* 556 F.2d 214 (3d Cir. 1977) (all protecting union authorization cards from disclosure). See also *American Federation of Government Employees v. U.S. Department of HHS,* 712 F.2d 931 (4th Cir. 1983) (protecting home addresses of nonunion employees from union request).
28. 5 U.S.C., 552(b).
29. *Arieff,* 712 F.2d at 1466.
30. See *Rose,* 425 U.S. at 375.
31. *Stern v. F.B.I.,* 737 F.2d 84, 91 (D. C. Cir. 1984).
32. *Rose,* 425 U.S. (release ordered after removal of identifying details).
33. *Harbolt v. Department of State,* 616 F.2d 772, 1774 (5th Cir. 1980) (records held exempt).
34. *Simpson v. Vance,* 648 F.2d 10 (D. C. Cir. 1980). But see *Department of State v. Washington Post Co.,* 456 U. S. at 602 n.5.
35. *National Prison Project of ACLU Foundation v. Sigler,* 390 F. Supp. 789 (D.D.C. 1975) (released, deletion of identifying details held sufficient).
36. *Church of Scientology v. Department of the Army,* 611 F.2d 738 (9th Cir. 1979) (held exempt).
37. *Swisher v. Department of the Air Force,* 495 F. Suppl. 369 (Wd. Mo. 1980), *aff'd,* 660 F.2d 269 (8th Cir. 1982) (held exempt).
38. *Heights Community Congress v. Veterans Administration,* 732 F.2d 526 (6th Cir. 1984) (held exempt).
39. *Rural Housing Alliance v. Department of Agriculture,* 502 F.2d 1179 (D. C. Cir. 1974) (remanded for balancing process).
40. *Simpson v. Vance,* 648 F.2d 10 (D. C. Cir. 1980) (released; not "similar file"). But see *Department of State v. Washington Post Co.,* 456 U.S. 595 (1982).
41. *Kurzon v. Dept. of Health and Human Services,* 649 F.2d 65 (1st Cir. 1981) (released due to public interest).
42. *Sims v. CIA,* 642 F.2d 562 (D. C. Cir. 1980).
43. *Poss v. NLRB,* 565 F.2d 654, 658 (10th Cir. 1977) (7)(c) case: "[t]he subject matter looks away from . . . privacy"). But see *Alirez v. NLRB,* 676 F.2d 423 (10th Cir. 1982) (similar records held exempt on stronger showing of potential harm).

44. *Getman v. NLRB,* 450 F.2d 670 (D. C. Cir. 1971) (released; privacy invasion "relatively minor"). But *cf American Federation of Government Employees v. U. S. Department of HSS,* 712 F.2d 931 (4th Cir. 1983) (protecting home addresses of nonunion employees from union request).
45. *Rose,* 425 U.S. at 372.
46. *I.B.E.W., Local 41 v. Dept. of HUD,* 763 F.2d 435 (D. C. Cir. 1985) at 436, citing *Washington Post v. Department of Health and Human Services,* 690 F.2d 252 (D. C. Cir. 1982) at 262.
47. *Arieff,* 712 F.2d at 1468-1469.
48. *Ferri v. Bell,* 645 F.2d 1213 (3d. Cir. 1981).
49. *National Association of Atomic Veterans v. Dir., Defense Nuclear Agency,* 583 F. Supp. 1483 (D.D.C. 1984). See also *Southern Utah Wilderness Alliance, Inc. v. Hodel,* 680 F. Supp. 37 (D.D.C. 1988) (court ruled that exemption 6 balance would not bar disclosure of Interior Department lists of names and addresses of persons who visited seven national parks where requester was nonprofit environmental group seeking to warn park users of environmental threats from nuclear waste dumps, coal strip-mining, and commercial development on public lands).
50. *Cochran v. United States,* 770 F.2d 949, 956 (11th Cir. 1985).
51. *Heights Community Congress v. Veterans Administration,* 732 F.2d 526 at 530, citing *Miller v. Bell,* 661 F.2d 623, 630 (7th Cir. 1981); *Brown v. FBI,* 658 F.2d 71, 76 (2d Cir. 1981). But see *I.B.E.W. Local U. No. 5 v. Department of HUD,* 852 F.2d 87, 91 (3d Cir. 1988) (questioning whether rejection of monitoring rationale can be reconciled with *Rose* view of FOIA's purpose "to open agency action to light of public scrutiny").
52. See, for example, *Minnis v. U.S. Department of Agriculture,* 737 F.2d 784 (9th Cir. 1984) at 787. See also *Marzen v. Department of HHS,* 852 F.2d 1148, 1153-54 (7th Cir. 1987) (despite existence of substantial public interest and extensive public record in "Infant Doe" discrimination case, medical records held exempt because "intimate details" of infant's deteriorating condition and conversations between his parents and doctors "would not appreciably serve the ethical debate" but would certainly cause anguish to parents).
53. *Wine Hobby U.S.A. v. I.R.S.,* 502 F.2d at 137. See also *Multnomah County Medical Soc. v. Scott,* 825 F.2d 1410, 1414 (9th Cir. 1987) (although the medical society performed an "educational service" by including information on changes in the

law, its mailing of a directory of physicians demonstrates that the society's motivation in requesting a list of names and addresses of Medicare beneficiaries was "overwhelmingly commercial"); *Minnis v. U.S. Department of Agriculture,* 737 F.2d 784, 786 (9th Cir. 1984) (asserted public interest in assessing fairness of procedure for granting river permits did not help lodge owner's commercial interest in list of permit applicants overcome applicants' privacy interest); *Professional Review Org. v. U.S. Department of Health,* 607 F. Suppl. 423 (D.D.C. 1985) (privacy interest in professional credentials and other personal information contained in requested resume prevails over requester's private commercial interest in protesting bid selection in related competitive procurement). But see *Aronson v. U.S. Dept. of HUD,* 822 F.2d 182, 185-86 (1st Cir. 1987) (requester's commercial motivation should not be considered in the balance because "Congress did not differentiate between the purposes for which information was requested").

54. See n.27, *supra.*
55. *Getman,* 450 F.2d 670 (D. C. Cir. 1971).
56. *Getman,* 450 F.2d at 675-76.
57. Rosenfeld, "The Freedom of Information Act's Privacy Exemption," 615.
58. *Getman,* 450 F.2d at 677 n.24.
59. Rosenfeld, "The Freedom of Information Act's Privacy Exemption," 615.
60. Ibid., 617.
61. *Robles v. Environmental Protection Agency,* 484 F.2d 843 (4th Cir. 1973).
62. *Robles,* 484 F.2d at 846-47.
63. *Kurzon,* 649 F.2d 65 (1st Cir. 1981).
64. Quoted in Information Commissioner, *Annual Report: 1984-85* (Ottawa: Minister of Supply and Services, 1985), 45.
65. See *Ditlow v. Shultz,* 517 F.2d 166 (D. C. Cir. 1975) at 170-71 and n.21.
66. See *Ditlow* 517 F.2d at 171-72; see also *American Federation of Government Employees,* 712 F.2d 931 (4th Cir. 1983); *Arieff,* 712 F.2d 1462 (D. C. Cir. 1983).
67. See, for example, *Washington Post Co. v. Department of HHS,* 690 F.2d at 263, 265 (Ethics in Government Act argues for disclosure of private employment and holdings of federal consultants); *Common Cause v. National Archives and Records Service,* 628 F.2d 179, 184-85 (D. C. Cir. 1980) (Federal Corrupt Practices Act policy of disclosure of campaign contributions); *Providence Journal Co. v. FBI,* 602 F.2d 1010 (1st Cir. 1979) at

1012-14 (wiretap act policy of nondisclosure of illegally obtained conversations determinative); *Congressional News Syndicate v. Department of Justice,* 438 F. Supp. 538 (D.D.C. 1977) at 543 (same as *Common Cause).*

68. See, for example, *Fund for Constitutional Government v. National Archives and Records Service,* 656 F.2d 856 (D. C. Cir. 1981) at 864-65; *Common Cause,* 628 F.2d at 184; *Congressional News Syndicate,* 438 F. Supp. at 543.

69. *Ackerly v. Ley,* 420 F.2d 1336, 1339-40 n.3 (D. C. Cir. 1969). Exemption 6 cases in accord include *Kurzon,* 649 F.2d at 69-70 (names of unsuccessful grant applicants not exempt notwithstanding regulations to the contrary); *Robles v. EPA,* 484 F.2d at 846; *Citizens for Environmental Quality v. U. S. Dept. of Agriculture,* 602 F. Supp. 534 (D.D.C. 1984) at 538; *Providence Journal Co. v. FBI,* 460 F. Supp. 762 (D.R.I. 1978) at 786; *Legal Aid Society of Alameda County v. Schultz,* 349 F. Supp. 771, 776 (N.D. Cal. 1972).

70. See *Poss v. NLRB,* 565 F.2d at 658 (10th Cir. 1977) (7 (c) case).

71. See *Von Tempske v. United States Department of HHS,* 1 G.D.S. Para. 82, 091 (W.D. Mo. 1981); *Radowich v. United States Attorney,* 501 F. Supp. 284, 288 (D. Md. 1980) *rev'd on other grounds,* 658 F.2d 71 (2d Cir. 1981) at 75.

72. *Kiraly v. FBI,* 728 F.2d 273 (6th Cir. 1984) at 279-80; *Brown v. FBI,* 658 F.2d 71 (2d Cir. 1981) at 75.

73. *Department of State v. Washington Post Co.,* 456 U.S. at 602 n.5.

74. Kimera Maxwell and Roger Reinsch, quoted in Richard F. Hixson, *Privacy in a Public Society* (New York: Oxford University Press, 1987), 201.

75. Ibid.

76. Rowe, "Privacy Legislation: Implications for Archivists" (see chapt. 2, n.2), 199.

77. Hixson, *Privacy in a Public Society,* 201.

78. Miller, *Assault on Privacy* (see chapt. 1, n.13), 154.

79. "Main Brief to the House of Commons Standing Committee on Justice and Legal Affairs from the Office of the Information Commissioner," May 7, 1986, sect.15.

80. An agency's ability to exercise a discretion to withhold records even after the individual concerned consents to their disclosure has been rejected by the Federal Court. See *The Information Commissioner v. Minister of Employment and Immigration,* May 2, 1986 (T.D.).

81. Information Commissioner, *Annual Report: 1986-87,* 34.

82. Treasury Board Secretariat, *Interim Policy Guide: Access to Information Act and The Privacy Act* (Ottawa: Minister of Supply and Services, 1983), 47.
83. Information Commissioner, *Annual Report: 1984-85,* 42.
84. Ibid., 44.
85. Treasury Board Secretariat, *Interim Policy Guide,* 49.
86. The head of the agency must consider whether disclosure may cause definite financial injury to the immediate family of the deceased; disclosure may endanger the physical wellbeing of the immediate family of the deceased; the head of the institution has reason to believe that an immediate family member or ex-spouse does not want the information released; the information contains medical, psychological or social work case reports or data which it is reasonable to believe would prove harmful to familial relationships; or, the deceased has expressed or implied any wishes with regard to the information. See Treasury Board Secretariat, *Interim Policy Guide,* 50-51.
87. *Access to Information Act,* S.C., 1980-81-82-83, c.111, 25.
88. Treasury Board Secretariat, *Interim Policy Guide,* 49.
89. Information Commissioner, *Annual Report: 1986-87,* 35 (File 171 (1/3)).
90. Ibid., 34.
91. Privacy Commissioner, *Annual Report: 1986-87,* 36-38.
92. See Information Commissioner, *Annual Report: 1984-85,* 44.
93. Ibid., 50.
94. See also Information Commissioner, *Annual Report: 1987-88,* 35-36 (file 0306) (disclosure of names and merit ranking of five teachers who lost their government jobs and were put on surplus list refused because public interest not sufficiently compelling); Information Commissioner, *Annual Report: 1985-86,* 62 (file 380) (disclosure of Employment and Immigrant files concerning the next-of-kin of a named deceased person to locate heirs refused).
95. See Treasury Board Secretariat, *Interim Policy Guide,* 50.
96. *Mary Bland v. National Capital Commission,* May 17, 1991 (T.D.).
97. Information Commissioner, *Annual Report: 1986-87,* 36.
98. Jean Pigott, NCC Chairman, quoted in *Bland* at 18.
99. *Bland* at 20.
100. Order-in-Council P.C. 1983-1668, cited in *Guidelines for the Disclosure of Personal Information for Historical Re-*

search at the *Public Archives of Canada* (Ottawa: Public Archives of Canada, 1983), 3.
  101. Ibid.
  102. Ibid., 4.
  103. Ibid., 5-6.
  104. In its interpretation of the language of section 3(1), "information relating to any discretionary benefit of a financial nature, including the granting of a license or permit, conferred on an individual, including the name of the individual and the exact nature of the benefit," the Federal Court has maintained that the discretionary benefit must be of a financial nature; licenses or permits that do not confer a financial benefit on the recipient, for example, seal hunt visitors permits, do not fall within the meaning of the provision. See *Information Commissioner v. The Minister of Fisheries and Oceans,* March 22, 1988, 20 F.T.R. 116, 50 D.L.R. (4th) 662. For the Information Commissioner's interpretation of "discretionary," see also Information Commissioner, *Annual Report: 1984-85,* 50 (files 1.84-139 (1/1), (2/2)).

  105. McCamus, "The Delicate Balance: Reconciling Privacy Protection with the Freedom of Information Principle" (see chapt. 2, n.66), 53.

  106. Bok, *Secrets* (see chapt. 1, n.51), 14.

  107. *Information Commissioner v. Minister of Employment and Immigration,* May 2, 1986 (T.D.).

  108. See "A Brief on the Revision of the Federal Access to Information and Privacy Acts (1982) for presentation to the Standing Committee on Justice and Legal Affairs of the House of Commons by the Task Force on Access to Information of the Social Science Federation of Canada," March 1986; "Brief from the Canadian Historical Association to the Standing Committee of Justice and Legal Affairs of the House of Commons concerning the Revision of the Access to Information and Privacy Act," 1986.

  109. Ralph R. Coram, "The Policies of Access to Historical Public Records in Post-War Britain, Canada and the United States: A Theoretical Perspective," Paper submitted to the Public Archives of Canada Course, September 1983, 40.

  110. Peter Dennis Bathory and Wilson Carey McWilliams, "Political Theory and the People's Right to Know," *Government Secrecy in Democracies,* ed. Itzhak Galnoor (New York: New York University Press, 1977), 8.

  111. Miller, *Assault on Privacy,* 156.

  112. Ronald Dworkin, *A Matter of Principle* (Cambridge, Mass.: Harvard University Press, 1985), 384.

113. Ibid., 388.

114. Ontario Commission on Freedom of Information and Individual Privacy, *Public Government for Private People,* vol. 2 (Toronto: Ministry of Government Services, 1980), 327.

115. After reviewing the statutory provisions against disclosure contained in Schedule II of the Access Act, the Standing Committee on Justice and Solicitor General has recommended that the statutory withholding provisions (section 24 and schedule II) of the Access to Information Act be repealed but that prohibitions already found in the Income Tax Act, the Statistics Act, and the Corporations and Labour Unions Returns Act be added to the Access to Information Act. See *Open and Shut: Enhancing the Right to Know and the Right to Privacy* (see chapt. 2, n. 49), Appendix B.

116. *Freedom of Information and Protection of Privacy Act,* 1987 S.O. 1987, c. 25.

117. Ontario Commission on Freedom of Information and Individual Privacy, *Public Government for Private People* vol. 2, 327.

118. The categories of personal information identified under the Ontario Act are essentially the same as those covered under the Canadian Act, with the addition of sexual orientation. See *Freedom of Information and Protection of Privacy Act,* 1987 S.O., 1987 c. 25, s.2.

119. *Freedom of Information and Protection of Privacy Act,* 1987 S.O. 1987 c. 25, s. 21(3).

120. For a description of the wide range of scientific research that is facilitated by access to government-held personal information, see, for example, David Flaherty, *Research and Statistical Uses of Ontario Government Personal Data* (Toronto: Commission on Freedom of Information and Individual Privacy, 1979); Flaherty, *Privacy and Government Data Banks: An International Perspective* (London: Mansell Publishing, 1979); Alan Westin, *Computers, Health Records and Citizens' Rights* (Washington, D. C.: National Bureau of Standards, December 1976), 300-303.

121. Harold Naugler, *The Archival Appraisal of Machine-Readable Records: A RAMP Study with Guidelines* (Paris: Unesco, 1984), 84.

122. Flaherty, *Research and Statistical Uses of Ontario Government Personal Data,* xviii.

123. Ibid., xiii.

124. Privacy Protection Study Commission, *Personal Privacy in an Information Society* (see chapt. 2, n.38), 570.

125. See E. C. Bryant and M. H. Hansen, "Invasion of Privacy and Surveys: A Growing Dilemma," in *Perspectives on Attitudes Assessment: Surveys and their Alternatives,* ed. H. W. Sinaiko and L. H. Broedling (Champaign, Ill.: Pendleton Publications, 1976), 68-77.

126. The eighteen Bellagio Principles are outlined in David H. Flaherty, "The Bellagio Conference on Privacy, Confidentiality and the Use of Governmental Microdata," *Secondary Analysis: New Direction for Program Evaluation,* ed. Robert F. Boruch (San Francisco: Jossey-Bass, 1978), 19-30.

127. However, the U. S. Privacy Protection Study Commission only gives agencies discretion to permit such cases, whereas the Ontario Act establishes access for research purposes as a matter of right.

128. Margaret L. Hedstrom, "Computers, Privacy, and Research Access to Confidential Information," *The Midwestern Archivist* 6 (1981): 5.

129. David Klassen, "The Provenance of Social Work Case Records: Implications for Archival Appraisal and Access," *Provenance* 1 (Spring 1983): 19.

Documenting the Lives of the Laboring and Unlettered

The Use of Archival Sources for Socio-Historical Research

> The toil, nay the most exciting toil of historians is to make dumb things speak.
> —Lucien Febvre[1]

Conflicts between privacy and access, as they relate to scholarly historical research specifically, have emerged in response to the sources and methods of such research. Increasingly, historians are drawn to explorations of society and societal processes that necessitate access to personal information held in government archives; and they frequently make use of methodologies that potentially threaten individual rights to privacy.

During the 1970s the numbers of academic users of archives increased dramatically.[2] In a statistical study of eleven countries, carried out for the Ninth International Congress on Archives in 1980, Michael Roper identified the main characteristics of current historical research that have impinged directly on the demand for access to archives. These have included the shift in interest to new branches of history and an enormous growth in the study of contemporary history dealing with the twentieth century and particularly the decades after World War I.[3] In addition, Roper points out, scholars from other academic disciplines have immersed themselves in the historical aspects of their subjects and have become historical geographers, historians of education, historians of science, technology and medicine, and so on. Others are using historical sources to enrich the study of their particular disciplines. The "applied historical studies" of social and political scientists, for example, are "'explorations of the past undertaken with the explicit purpose of advancing social scientific enquiries'... in which historical data are used to test hypotheses of general application."[4]

The involvement of nonhistorians in the study of historical data has led to what Roper describes as, "a considerable cross-fertilisation between history and other disciplines as a consequence of which historians have adopted and adapted the techniques of those disciplines ... to develop new approaches to historical studies."[5] The new techniques and approaches are demonstrated most dramatically in the so-called "new" social history—which has emerged over the last twenty years as a dominant genre in historical research. The new social history, which has revitalized certain traditional subdisciplines and spawned new ones, among them, working class history, ethnic history, black history, women's history, urban and rural history, family history, and so on, each with distinct interests, methodologies, and journals—is generally considered the fastest growing field of historical research.[6]

Social history owes much to the total history concept of the French *Annales* school with its balanced emphasis on social structure, cultural values and physical environment.[7] The *Annales* movement was launched in 1929 with the founding of the journal *Annales d'histoire economique et sociale,* by Marc Bloch and Lucien Febvre. Rejecting the dominant pattern of nineteenth century historical writing associated with the German scientific school, which centered on the study of elites governing the nation-states, *Annales* scholars insisted on a "broadened and deepened history," one which went below politics to the fundamental causes of stability and change.[8] A central frame of reference for *Annales* scholars was demography—the life conditions of communities of people as revealed in statistics of births, deaths, and diseases. Under the influence of the demographic view of society, the notion of history as the record of growth, conflict, and destruction, and the powerful actions of certain men, gave way to history as "the record of the expression of demographically significant preferences; the lunge of demography *here* as opposed to *there*."[9]

By rejecting traditional history, *Annales* scholars rejected, too, the "narrow documentary base" on which that history was built.[10] The *Annales* methodology favored structural analyses of the economic and material conditions of past societies. As Tom Nesmith has observed, "the ambition to master a wider range of sources led followers of Bloch and Febvre to rationalize their research methods using technology and quantitative procedures."[11] *Annales* scholars collected and analyzed large quantities of data from a wide range of sources—architectural remains, land records, birth, marriage, and death registers, tax records, wills, account books, marriage settlements, to name only a few—spanning generations and even centuries. From this greatly expanded documentary base, *Annales* historians assembled the "parahistoric languages" of demography, technology, money, towns, that had traditionally been kept separate from each other and consigned to the margins of history.[12] From these parahistoric languages there emerged a broad picture of society "from the bottom up," a picture that emphasized the living conditions and collective mentality of the majority.

The *Annales* approach has exercised a significant influence on the new social history that has emerged in the last twenty years. The newness of this social history refers mainly to the use by some social historians of concepts from the social sciences and specifically the enthusiasm for quantitative methods, which have been applied primarily to demographic and social mobility studies. Originally developed in the mid-nineteen-sixties to analyze and record numerous variables such as opinion polls and voting behavior, quantitative research methods and statistical sampling techniques involve the analysis of huge quantities of economic, social, and political data. At its simplest level, quantitative research is the counting and comparing of that which can be counted and compared.[13] Implicit in this definition is the measurement of phenomena—directly or indirectly observable—to which numbers are assigned according to specified rules. The data base of numeric documentation thus created can then be subjected to computerized statistical analysis.

When the first historical studies of demography and social mobility based on quantitative analyses of manuscript census returns, city directories, and parish registers appeared in the late sixties and early seventies, reviewers suggested that social history "would lend a healthy depth and precision to more traditionally based enquiries into the lives of the laboring and 'unlettered' during the nineteenth century."[14] The perspective on society is a stratigraphic one,[15] built largely from quantified data upon a base of demographic information. Census enumerations and parish registers have, for the most part, provided the backbone of demographic studies; but, as Andre LaRose's annual bibliography of historical demography makes clear, a variety of other evidence is also available, largely in the form of routinely generated administrative records: assessment rolls, land records, military records, marriage contracts, school records, hospital records, criminal records, bank records, ships' nominal rolls, and the records of benevolent associations.[16]

In Canada, one of the most ambitious projects in the area of historical demography is being undertaken at the Université de Montréal, where scholars in the Programme de Recherche en Démographie Historique have been attempting to reconstitute the entire population of Québec from 1608 to 1850. Relying primarily on parish registers and nominal census data, the project aims at eventually producing a demographic biography of every individual "qui ont mis le pied sur la territoire québecois" up to the mid-nineteenth century.[17] A similar project is underway at the Société de Recherche sur les Populations at the Université de Québec à Chicoutimi. Since 1972, a team of demographers has been engaged in building a comprehensive data bank of the population of the Saguenay-Lake St. John area from 1838 up to 1931. The data base, which includes parish registers, manuscript census data, employment records, and other routinely generated records, supports studies by demographers, sociologists, and medical researchers, as well as historians and other scholars.[18] Other data bases established for the purposes of historical demography include the Philadelphia Social History Project at the University of Pennsylvania, established by Theodore Hershberg in 1972[19], and the Hamilton Project.[20]

Demographic analysis furthers the broader aim of social history to describe the "historical meaning of social reality."[21] The focus is on "the constituent elements of society: class, gender, family, local or regional communities, and occupational, ethnic, and age groups."[22] Over the last twenty years, social history has examined the sources and consequences of social discontinuity in a wide variety of social groups, among them, women, children, adolescents, and the elderly; voluntary associations; political factions; professional and vocational groups; crowds and movements; social classes; and local populations.[23]

The impact of industrialization on the social conditions of the working class and on the working class culture has been one area of extensive analysis.[24] In the United States, social historians have also studied the effect of urbanization on the Black American family. In a study by Janice Reiff, Michel Dahlin, and Daniel Scott Smith, for example, manuscript census returns between 1880 and 1900 were used to track a representative sample of black urban immigrants who moved to southern cities after the Civil War and created the first large-scale urban black culture in the United States.[25] Census-analysis techniques have also been applied to studies of several nineteenth-century urban and rural communities.[26]

The experiences of families in given communities, as well as families of particular social, racial, and ethnic groups, have provided social historians with a wealth of information concerning the adaptation and preservation of group structures and values over time. Social historical analysis approaches the family "as the lowest common denominator of demographic and social structural analysis, in effect, a laboratory for the study of the processes of social discontinuity in larger populations."[27] By tracing individuals through, for example, parish registers, census returns, birth, death, and marriage registers, assessment and other property records, researchers can "reconstitute" the family process in specific communities.[28]

The perspective promoted by this record-linking technique is a longitudinal one. Historians active in the field have generated a complex picture of the effects of social change on the structure, function, and culture of family life as well as the adaptive strategies employed by families to promote continuity in the face of change. The central concern of these studies is, in David Gagan's estimation, "the larger framework of local, regional and national economics which determined the nature of economic opportunity in the past and, therefore, the sources and timing of social discontinuity which is revealed, at the microcosmic level of family life, as a process of adaptation to quantum shifts in the material bases of life."[29]

Family-centered social history has also facilitated investigations into the actual living conditions of specific family members such as women, children, and adolescents. Women's history, specifically, attempts to document the hitherto hidden areas of life in which women have traditionally been active and to explore the public institutions that have assumed family functions, among them, prisons, hospitals, schools, and public and private welfare organizations. Carroll Smith Rosenberg observes that social historians, and historians of women especially, focus their concern on "private places: the household, the family, the bed, the nursery, and kinship systems." Demographic sources have proven essential to such studies:

> Census and other statistical data can help delineate the lives of such women: the proportion of females to males and the female mortality rate for various age groups; the numbers who married, divorced, were widowed or deserted, and at what ages; the number of children per

mother and their mortality; how many women were emplyed, in what kinds of jobs, for how much pay—and so forth. Company personnel records, reform school, prison, court, hospital, and morgue records, when they exist and are available, will all yield useful information.[30]

The history of women in the workplace and in the professions has been examined as well by a number of social historians.[31]

In an attempt to "illuminat[e] the texture of life among the 'submerged' four-tenths"[32] of society, many social historians have focused their gaze on prisons, hospitals, mental asylums, homes for wayward girls, poor farms, reform school, and a number of other public and philanthropic institutions dedicated to various forms of social welfare, as a means of determining the dominant assumptions of these institutions and their impact on client populations as well as the society at large.[33] To pursue their investigations, many historians have turned to the case files generated by such agencies as a valuable source of documentation on the lives of the historically inarticulate.

The case files of public and private social-welfare agencies contain highly detailed information on persons, groups, and institutions, rarely recorded elsewhere, and are considered particularly useful in reconstructing life histories and identifying and explaining social processes. G. J. Parr's study of the orphaned, deserted, and dependent children who emigrated to Canada in the late nineteenth and early twentieth century, *Labouring Children: British Immigrant Apprentices to Canada, 1869-1924* [34] is one example of this approach to social history. Drawing on information gleaned largely from case files, particularly those preserved on former wards of Dr. Barnardo's Homes, the British agency that dominated the juvenile immigration program in the late nineteenth and early twentieth century, Parr has constructed a highly detailed picture of the material conditions of life among the child emigrants who were the object of a significant "evangelical rescue" movement of that period.

Historians view the case files of public and private welfare agencies as a valuable source of information for documenting a stratum of society which traditionally has been poorly represented in written sources. According to R. Joseph Anderson:

> The historical value of these records results from the fact that the case method, as employed in contemporary public welfare systems, has remained essentially investigatory since its origin among the late nineteenth-century charity organization societies. The societies' "friendly visitors" sought to diagnose and treat poverty as a character defect rather than as a social problem, and this approach led to the creation of individualized profiles of recipients, which documented their habits, attitudes, and lifestyles as well as their economic means ... and, until the early 1970s, they continued to combine normative judgments and objective information.[35]

Social welfare case files contain a wide range of quantitative and anecdotal information on the personal adjustment, family dynamics, and social functioning of welfare clients; moreover, since "public welfare agencies frequently serve as referral sources and focal contacts for other service organizations. . . . [the] records often contain information from schools, clinics, rehabilitation programs, private charities, and other community agencies."[36] Discussing her own use of case files, G. J. Parr suggests that they are a necessary source of documentation on the lives of ordinary men and women because of the limitations of census data and literary sources: "There are too many important questions which the census-taker never asks, too many reasons to suspect the typicality of the laboring man or woman of literary inclinations."[37] She predicts that the usefulness of personal case files to social historians will "increase exponentially" in the future because, although case files

> demand a severe sacrifice in breadth by comparison with census, assessment or parish records, the narrow-

ing of focus allows for considerable sharpening in detail. ... With the information which beadles, bailiffs and the benevolent felt necessary to manage the life of an inmate or applicant, a social historian can craft a collective biography which supplements the depth of the census and the breadth of the literary sources, adding a dimension heretofore available through neither. [38]

A recent American study of the use of archival sources in social history research, undertaken by Frederic Miller,[39] bears out Parr's prediction. Miller analyzed the use of archival records in 214 scholarly articles on social history published between 1981 and 1985. He found that, in process-oriented articles, that is, articles that analyzed social processes, structures, and long-term change, fifty per cent of all the series used[40] were quantifiable records, including case files, public censuses, and vital records. Moreover, the intensity of use of case files and related records was high; one half of all the series fundamental to, and cited in, articles on specific population groups or social and demographic structure were case files, census records, and related materials.

Given these findings, Miller has theorized that the most likely developments in social history may be

> [an] increased use of the kinds of records now heavily used in research on the 1860-1900 period for research on the 1900-1945 period . . . [This is] an inevitable consequence of the regular release of the census and similar public records and of case files, all of which are now used intensively in research on the nineteenth century. . . . The census and case level information that will become available for the early twentieth century probably will be used as intensively as it has been for research on the previous period. [41]

Historians initially concerned with social mobility and working class life in the early industrial period already have begun to pursue their investigations well into the twentieth century. [42]

Not surprisingly, the enormous amount of individually identifiable information maintained in government recordkeeping systems is considered a valuable source of raw, quantifiable data for social historical analysis. And, increasingly, historians are relying on archivists to preserve substantial amounts of this raw data and make it available for research. Such demands place archivists in an ambivalent position, for although the detailed records created by government agencies have undoubted research value and will increasingly come into the jurisdiction of archivists, the information contained in such records clearly falls within areas of life designated as private and their disclosure constitutes an intrusion into the privacy of countless citizens. Jean Tener expresses the dilemma thus:

> as scholars turn from the biographical details of the politically important to the materials of quantitative history, the privacy endangered is that of ordinary citizens "who may be unable to assert their rights because they are legally incompetent (children or institutionalized persons) or because they are unaware that records involving them" have been transferred to private or public archives.[43]

The multiple uses to which personal information could be put by researchers raises another worrisome prospect: that, once such information leaves the custody of the archives (in copy form), archivists will be powerless to protect it from further disclosure(s), either inadvertent or deliberate, or to prevent it being combined with other sorts of personal information, deposited in a research data base, and used for different purposes than those agreed to at the time the information was originally disclosed by the archives.

Personal case files are perhaps the most prevalent type of confidential documentation maintained by government agencies.[44] The personal case files of public welfare agencies, for example, include a great deal of sensitive personal information, as Virginia Stewart describes:

the case record may include age, sex, religious preference, medical history, legal and financial status, marriage, family and social relationships, and residence and employment patterns, all of which may be supplemented by test results, investigations, diagnoses, and notations of courses of therapy or intervention.[45]

An American survey undertaken in 1973 found that case record series occurred in a wide range of archival collections, including records of public and private welfare agencies; clinics, hospitals, and public health agencies; juvenile homes and residential and special schools; adoption agencies; and labor union grievance and compensation boards.[46] Peter Gillis has identified similar collections of personal, investigatory, and report case files created by the numerous departments and agencies of the Canadian government. The Canada Employment and Immigration Commission, for example, has generated at least ten separate and identifiable case file series, including unemployment and insurance benefit claims, unemployment insurance complaints, unemployment insurance prosecutions, canadian manpower mobility program files, training-on-the-job files, local initiative program files, immigration case files, chinese case files, special case files and deportation case files.[47] As Gillis notes, it is clear that "the concept of privacy is a vital part of the administrative context in which such information is solicited ... Individuals, corporations, organizations, and groups are discussed and expose themselves in these files in a very intimate and usually frank manner."[48]

From the historical researcher's vantage point, the availability of such records "will greatly expand the range of both traditionally minded scholars and cliometricians by bridging their approaches to working class culture and society";[49] and, they argue, while the preservation of, and the administration of access to, records containing sensitive personal information presents serious problems for archivists because of their confidentiality, the individual's right to privacy "must be balanced by the collective need to understand society and society's needs."[50] Government records serve accountability,[51] a point that is emphasized in the report of the U.S. Committee on the Records of Government:

> Government records have a unique character that imposes special responsibilities on the agencies that preserve and manage them. Government is the one institution that in one way or another touches the lives of every individual within its jurisdiction. It not only affects the lives of all citizens, but inherent in that contact between government and citizen is a complex interdependence of rights and obligations, of mutual responsibility and accountability. The records of this most fundamental of human institutions therefore partake of a fundamentality of their own in respect to it. [52]

The records of various public welfare agencies, for example, which contain a great deal of sensitive personal information, reflect a number of important social values; among them, the obligation of the state to improve the social welfare of its citizens and its accountability for the provision of such services. The sensitive nature of such records should not deter archivists from appraising the records to determine whether they should be preserved and, if they are to be preserved, arranging for their eventual transfer to archival custody.

Nevertheless, when archivists assume custody over records containing personal information and take responsibility for administering access to them, two social values—the individual's need for privacy and society's need to understand itself—are brought into potential conflict. On the one hand, as custodians of these records, archivists are obliged to safeguard the integrity of the privacy interests represented in them; on the other, as communicators of society's documentary memory, they are obliged to promote access to records to the fullest extent possible. The question is, how is the balance to be struck?

Archivists have traditionally safeguarded individual privacy while ensuring that records containing personal information are eventually made available for research through the application of closed periods. At the beginning of the nineteenth century, most western countries accepted the principle that public documents might be made available on the expiry of a set time-limit which would vary according to the categories of document. The passage of time principle "assumes that the reasons for and appropriateness of denying access diminish over time. Or, to put it another way, the public interest in permitting access to government records increases over time."[53] Closed periods are an essential means of ensuring that records of permanent value are eventually made publicly available for research. In the absence of formally fixed restricted periods, many classes of records containing personal information might remain in limbo indefinitely. But how long should records containing personal information be protected from public disclosure?

In 1972, under the auspices of Unesco, the International Council on Archives (ICA) published a draft law on production and right of access, the intention of which was to bring archival legislation "into line with the political, legal, and technical exigencies of modern development."[54] Under the draft law, records containing information that might violate either personal privacy or state secrets would be opened to the public 50 years "after the conclusion of the matter to which they refer." In his assessment of the ICA draft law, David Klassen rightly concludes that, given the value which contemporary society attaches to personal privacy, "it is inconceivable that such standards will be enacted legislatively or adhered to voluntarily by records creators in the foreseeable future."[55] To date, revisions to the draft law or alternative proposals for closed periods have not been forthcoming.

Although formal statements of access principles have been developed by a number of professional associations, they do not offer much assistance to archivists attempting to determine an acceptable period of closure for records that implicate privacy values. *The Standards for Access to Research Materials in Archival and Manuscript Repositories* issued by the Council of the Society of American Archivists (SAA) in 1973, for example, confirms the principle of specified time restrictions, but it fails to make any recommendations with respect to the appropriate duration of closed periods.[56] The SAA's Code of Ethics is similarly vague in its advocacy of "clearly stated restrictions of limited duration."[57]

In practice, there is little uniformity in statutory or other (e.g., administrative) rules and procedures governing closed periods. Provisions for specified time restrictions vary considerably, depending on the recordkeeping environment in which the personal information is collected and maintained. For many classes of records, provisions for eventual access after a period of time are nonexistent. Records containing some of the most sensitive kinds of personal information, for example, case files, usually are either retained for a relatively short period of time and destroyed or simply not transferred to the archives.[58] When time restrictions are specified either by legislation, regulation, or administrative policy, the duration of closed periods for records containing personal information is usually tied to the life expectancy of the individual to whom the information relates, in recognition of the common law principle that the right to personal privacy does not diminish significantly over the lifetime of an individual. The U.S. National Archives and Records Administration closes records that contain sensitive personal information, the disclosure of which would constitute a "clearly unwarranted invasion of privacy" for 75 years after the events to which the records relate; "a figure arrived at with reference to actuarial tables."[59] The state archives of Georgia and Indiana also operate under a 75-year rule. In Canada, on the other hand, the protection of personal information held in government archives covered by omnibus data protection legislation is tied to birth and death dates, rather than to the events to which the information relates; and the protection is extended for a number of years beyond the death of the individual, ranging from 10 years after death to 30 years after death.[60]

On the whole, the archival profession has been disinclined to advocate access policies that extend the right to privacy beyond an individual's death. A 1986 Roundtable on Access to Information and Privacy sponsored by the ICA, for example, recommended that "legislation and archival practice should not prevent or unduly delay historical research by extending the protection of privacy to deceased persons." Similarly, the commentary accompanying the SAA Code of Ethics notes that "privacy concerns only living persons."[61] But does the right to privacy always terminate upon the death of the individual to whom the information relates? Some philosophers argue that people's notions of themselves can extend beyond their physical limits. This "extension of self" is a complex phenomenon: Is information about an individual's family information about that individual? Stanley Benn suggests that in cases involving disclosures about parents, children, or siblings, the "extension of self" may be based on a feeling of responsibility for, or identification with, the other person.[62]

By extending the protection of individual privacy beyond the life of the individual to whom the information relates, Canadian data protection laws implicitly recognize the validity of the right to privacy after death. Such a right is also recognized in most old laws governing access to archives, which included provisions to protect "family honor"; many of these provisions continue to exist, particularly in archival legislation in Latin America. According to Michel Duchein, "in many countries, the law expressly states that the notion of protecting private life includes not only living persons but also the memory of the dead and their families":[63]

> The negative consequences of revealing an illegitimate birth, for example, may affect the descendants of a family several generations later. Likewise, the disclosure of an impropriety committed in the past can be seriously damaging to the perpetrator's descendants and family even long after his death.[64]

In U.S. FOIA cases, courts have been split in construing the personal privacy interest under exemption 7(c), relating to law enforcement and investigatory records, on whether such privacy interest lapses upon the death of the individual.[65] Four states now permit lawsuits based on the right to privacy after death. Claims of invasion of privacy have been made on such grounds, for example, in cases where the "victim" never chose to enter public life.[66] Given the current uncertainty about the appropriate duration of closed periods, there is clearly a need for the archival community, through its professional organizations, to develop guidelines for closed periods attuned to the diverse kinds of personal information in archival custody; and for archivists to lobby for statutory and regulatory amendments, where these are required, to implement those guidelines.

Of course, establishing (or advocating) coherent policies and procedures for the administration of closed periods addresses only one dimension of the access-privacy problem facing archivists. Closed periods allow for the eventual availability of records containing personal information; they do not offer archivists any guidance on administering limited access to records that fall within closed periods. Lengthy time restrictions, without some provision for limited access, are generally considered unacceptable to both the research and the archival communities, because they would severely restrict the research that could be done on contemporary social issues by rendering whole classes of records definitively inaccessible for research. The ICA has endorsed the principle of special clearance procedures on the grounds that they are essential for documents closed for extended periods of time.[67]

On the whole, the principle has been easier to defend than to apply. Although administrative and technical procedures for allowing access to records containing personal information have been developed in many archives, in many others such procedures are either nonexistent or *ad hoc* at best. The administration of access to records containing personal information has been severely hampered by the often confusing recordkeeping environments that government archivists find themselves in, as we shall discover in the next chapter.

Notes

1. Quoted by Carlo Paganini, "Interventions," in *Archivum: International Review of Archives,* 29, Proceedings of the International Congress on Archives, London, 15-19 September, 1980 (Munich: K. G. Saur, 1982): 65.

2. The Public Archives of Canada documented a 71 percent growth in the number of academic users between 1971 and 1976; The Archives generales du Royaume and Archives de l'Etat of Belgium documented a 39 percent increase over the same period. In Spain, the growth in the period 1957-75 was 757 percent; in the United Kingdom, between 1962-78, the growth documented was 558 percent. At the U. S. National Archives, non-genealogist researchers represented 43 percent of all research conducted in 1976. See Michael Roper, "The Academic Use of Archives," *Archivum,* 29: 42-43, table 3.

3. In 1971, the entries in *Historical Abstracts* dealing with pre-1914 history numbered 3303 as compared to 3103 entries dealing with post-1914 history; in 1976, there were 4100 entries dealing with pre-1914 history and 4994 entries dealing with post-1914 history. See Roper, "Academic Use of Archives," 40, table 1.

4. Roper, "Academic Use of Archives," 28. For a more detailed discussion of the expansion of clientele of archives, see Ivan Borsa, "The Expanding Archival Clientele in the Post-World War II Period," in *Archivum: International Review of Archives,* 26, Proceedings of the 8th International Congress on Archives, Washington, 27 September-1 October 1976 (Munich: K. G. Saur, 1979): 119-26.

5. Roper, "Academic Use of Archives," 28.

6. Dale C. Mayer, "The New Social History: Implications for Archivists," *American Archivist* 48 (Fall 1985): 388.

7. For a detailed analysis of the *Annales* school and its influence, see Troian Stoianovich, *French Historical Method: The Annales Paradigm* (Ithaca, N.Y.: Cornell University Press, 1976).

8. Marc Bloch, quoted by Tom Nesmith in "Le Roy Ladurie's 'Total History' and Archives," *Archivaria* 12 (Summer 1981): 128.

9. George W. S. Trow, *Within the Context of No-Context* (Boston: Little, Brown, 1981), 314.

10. Nesmith, "Le Roy Ladurie's 'Total History'," 128.

11. Ibid.

12. Fernand Braudel, *The Structures of Everyday Life: The Limits of the Possible,* vol. 1 of *Civilization and Capitalism, 15th-18th Century,* trans. Sian Reynolds (New York: Harper and Row, 1981), 27.

13. Charles M. Dollar, "Quantitative History and Archives," in *Archivum,* 29: 46.

14. G. J. Parr, "Case Records as Sources for Social History," *Archivaria* 4 (Summer 1977): 122. As Parr notes, among the most enduring of the earlier enquiries, i.e., those that have continued to exercise a profound influence on social historians, particularly historians of the working class, are E. P. Thompson, *The Making of the English Working Class* (London: Gollancz, 1963); Eric Hobsbawm, *Laboring Men* (London: Weidenfeld and Nicolson, 1964); and Hobsbawm, *Primitive Rebels* (New York: Norton, 1965).

15. The word *stratigraphic* is used by Emmanuel Le Ray Ladurie in *The Territory of the Historian* to encapsulate his conception of rural civilization. Cited in Nesmith in "Le Roy Ladurie's 'Total History'," 129.

16. Listed in Chad Gaffield, "Theory and Method in Canandian Historical Demography," *Archivaria* 14 (Summer 1982): 129.

17. Gagan, David, and H. E. Turner, "Social History in Canada: A Report on the State of the Art," *Archivaria* 14 (Summer 1982): 36. A major work that has emerged from the Université de Montréal demography project is Hubert Charbonneau's *Vie et mort de nos ancêtres: étude démographique* (Montréal: Les Presses de l'Université de Montréal, 1975).

18. Examples of studies that have been conducted using the Saquenay Project database include Chad M. Gaffield, "Canadian Families in Cultural Context: Hypotheses from the Mid-Nineteenth Century," CHA *Historical Papers* (1979): 48-70; Bettina Bradbury, "The Family Economy and Work in an Industrializing City: Montreal in the 1870s," CHA *Historical Papers* (1979): 71-96.

19. Studies that have come out of the Philadelphia Social History Project are reported in Theodore Hershberg, ed., *Philadelphia: Work, Space, Family and Group Experience in the Nineteen Century: Essays Toward an Interdisciplinary History of the City* (Oxford: Oxford University Press, 1981).

20. The Hamilton Project database was generated for the purpose of studying the social structure of a nineteenth-century Canadian city, Hamilton, Ontario. The database used mainly census records and assessment rolls at decade intervals. A major study based on the Hamilton Project is Michael Katz's *The*

People of Hamilton, Canada West: Family and Class in the Mid-Nineteenth Century (Cambridge, Mass.: Harvard University Press, 1975).

21. Gagan and Turner, "Social History in Canada," 27.

22. Nesmith, "Archives from the Bottom Up: Social History and Archival Scholarship," *Archivaria* 14 (Summer 1982): 9.

23. Gagan and Turner, "Social History in Canada," 27.

24. See, for example, Herbert Gutman, *Work, Culture and Society in Industrializing America: Essays in American Working Class and Social History* (New York: Knopf, 1976); Alan Dawley and Paul Faler, "Cultural Aspects of the Industrial Revolution: Lynn, Massachusetts, Shoemakers and Industrial Morality, 1826-1860," *Labor History* 15 (1974): 367-94; G. Kealey and P. Warrian, eds., *Essays in Canadian Working Class History* (Toronto: McClelland and Stewart, 1976); Brian Palmer, *A Culture in Conflict: Skilled Workers and Industrial Capitalism in Hamilton, Ontario, 1860-1914* (Montreal: McGill-Queen's Press, 1979).

25. Janice L. Reiff, Michel R. Dahlen, and Daniel Scott Smith, "Rural Push and Urban Pull: Work and Family Experiences of Older Black Women in Southern Cities, 1880-1900," *Journal of Social History* 16 (Summer 1983): 39-48. See also Daniel Scott Smith, "A Community Based Sample of the Older Population from the 1880 and 1900 United States Manuscript Census," *Historical Methods* 11 (1978): 67-74; D. S. Smith, Michel Dahlen, and Mark Friedberger, "The Family Structures of the Older Black Population in the American South in 1880 and 1900," *Sociology and Social Research* 63 (1979): 55.

26. See, for example, Stephan Thernstom, *Poverty and Progress: Social Mobility in a Nineteenth-Century City* (Cambridge, Mass.: Harvard University Press, 1964), and *The Other Bostonians: Poverty and Progress in the American Metropolis, 1880-1970* (Cambridge, Mass.: Harvard University Press, 1973); Michael B. Katz, *The People of Hamilton, Canada West: Family and Class in a Mid-Nineteenth Century City* (Cambridge, Mass.: Harvard University Press, 1975); Tamara Harevan and Rudolph Langenenbach, *Amoskeag: Life and Work in an American Factory-City* (New York: Pantheon Books, 1978); David Gagan, *Hopeful Travellers: Families, Land and Social Change in Mid-Victorian Peel County, Canada West* (Toronto: University of Toronto Press, 1981).

27. Gagan and Turner, "Social History in Canada," 30.

28. Gaffield, "Theory and Method in Canadian Historical Demography," 125.

29. Gagan and Turner, "Social History in Canada," 32.
30. Eva S. Moseley, "Sources for the 'New Women's History'," *American Archivist* 43 (Spring 1980): 182.
31. See, for example, Milton Cantor and Bruce Laurie, eds., *Class, Sex, and the Woman Worker* (Westport, Conn.: Greenwood Press, 1977); Thomas Dublin, *Women at Work: The Transformation of Work and Community in Lowell, Massachusetts, 1826-1869* (New York: Columbia University Press, 1979); Barbara J. Harris, *Beyond her Sphere: Women and the Professions in American History* (Westport, Conn.: Greenwood Press, 1978); Veronica Strong-Boag, "Canada's Women Doctors: Feminism Constrained," in *A Not Unreasonable Claim: Women and Reform in Canada, 1880s-1920s,* ed. Linda Kealey (Toronto: The Women's Press, 1979); Alison Prentice and Susan Laskin, *Family, School and Society in Nineteenth Century Canada* (Toronto: Oxford University Press, 1975).
32. G. J. Parr, "Case Records as Sources," 122.
33. See, for example, Joan Jacobs Brumberg, "Ruined Girls: Changing Community Responses to Illegitimacy in Upstate New York, 1890-1920," *Journal of Social History* 18 (Winter 1984): 247-63; Glenn C. Altschuler and Jan M. Saltzgaber, "Clearinghouse for Paupers: The Poor Farm of Seneca County, New York, 1830-1860," *Journal of Social History* 17 (Summer 1984): 573-600; Steven Ruggles, "Fallen Women: The Inmates of the Magdalen Society Asylum of Philadelphia, 1836-1908," *Journal of Social History* 16 (Summer 1983): 65-82.
34. G. J. Parr, *Labouring Children: British Child Immigrants to Canada, 1868-1924* (London: Croom Helm, 1980).
35. R. Joseph Anderson, "Public Welfare Case Records: A Study of Archival Practices," *American Archivist* 43 (Spring 1980): 165.
36. Anderson, "Public Welfare Case Records," 169.
37. Parr, "Case Records as Sources," 123.
38. Ibid.
39. Frederic Miller, "Use, Appraisal, and Research: A Case Study of Social History," *American Archivist* 49 (Fall 1986): 371-92.
40. In Miller's study, each district and identifiable set of files was counted as a series.
41. Miller, "Use, Appraisal and Research," 389.
42. See, for example, Stephan Thernstrom, *The Other Bostonians*; Michael Weber, *Social Change in an Industrial Town: Patterns of Progress in Warren, Pennsylvania from the Civil War to World War I* (University Park, Penna.: Pennsylvania State

University Press, 1976); Tamara K. Harevan and Randolph Langenbach, *Amoskeag: Life and Work in an American Factory-City.*

43. Jean Tener, "Accessibility and Archives," (see chapt. 2, n. 19), 28.

44. The archival literature on confidentiality issues related to public welfare case files in the United States has grown since the publication of Virginia Stewart's ground-breaking article, "Problems of Confidentiality in the Administration of Personal Case Records," *American Archivist* 37 (1974): 387-97. Since that time, the issue has been addressed in a number of articles, including R. Joseph Anderson, "Public Welfare Case Records: A Study of Archival Practices," *American Archivist* 43 (Spring 1980): 169-79; Roland M. Baumann, "The Administration of Access to Confidential Records in State Archives: Common Practices and the Need for a Model Law," *American Archivist* 49 (Fall 1986): 349-70; David Klassen, "The Provenance of Social Work Case Records: Implications for Archival Appraisal and Access," *Provenance* 1 (Spring 1983): 5-39; Alice Robbin, "State Archives and Issues of Personal Privacy: Policies and Practices," *American Archivist* 49 (Spring 1986): 163-75.

In Canada, the literature on public welfare case files in not as well developed. The two articles that have become standard reading on the subject are: G. J. Parr, "Case Records as Sources for Social History," *Archivaria* 4 (Summer 1979): 122-36; and Peter Gillis, "The Case File: Problems of Acquisition and Access from the Federal Perspective," *Archivaria* 6 (Summer 1978): 32-39.

45. Stewart, "Problems of Confidentiality in Administration of Personal Case Records," 387.

46. Ibid., 391.

47. Gillis, "The Case File: Problems of Acquisition and Access," 33.

48. Ibid., 38.

49. Parr, "Case Records as Sources," 136.

50. Allan Bogue, "Data Dilemmas: Quantitative History and the Social Science History Association," *Social Science History* 3 (October 1979): 212.

51. David Bearman, quoted in David B. Gracy, "Is there a future in the use of archives?" *Archivaria* 24 (Summer 1987): 8.

52. "Appendix III-D, Principles for State Archival and Records Management Agencies," *Committee on the Records of Government Report* (Washington, D. C.: March 1985), 170.

53. Robert Craig Brown, "Government and Historian: A Perspective on Bill C43," *Archivaria* 13 (Winter 1981-82): 121.
54. Quoted in Tener, "Accessibility and Archives," 18.
55. Klassen, "Provenance of Social Work Case Files," 21-22.
56. In Sue E. Holbert, *Archives and Manuscripts: Reference and Access* (Chicago: Society of American Archivists, 1977), Appendix 1.
57. *American Archivist* 43 (Summer 1980): 414.
58. Jean Tener, "Accessibility and Archives," 29.
59. Klassen, "Provenance of Social Work Case Records," 21. The U. S. Bureau of the Census's prohibition on disclosure of raw census information for 72 years after the taking of the census is also based on the life expectancy of census subjects.
60. At the federal level, records containing personal information are not open until 20 years after the death of the individual to whom the information pertains; in Manitoba, records containing personal information are opened 10 years after the individual's death; Ontario opens them 30 years after death. Similar protection is extended to raw census information, which Statistics Canada closes for 92 years after the taking of the census. The 1901 census, which will be opened in 1993, may be the last census that Statistics Canada will release in individually identifiable form, due to the provisions of the Statistics Act.
61. *American Archivist* 43 (Summer 1980): 416.
62. Stanley Benn, "Privacy, Freedom, and Respect for Persons," *Nomos XIII: Privacy,* ed. J. R. Pennock and J. W. Chapman (New York: Atherton Press, 1971), 12-13.
63. Duchein, *Obstacles to Access, Use and Transfer of Information,* 22.
64. Ibid., 21.
65. Compare *Diamond v. FBI,* 707 F.2d 75, 77-78 (2d Cir. 1983) (death or voluntary disclosure "so diminished any privacy interest as to amount to a 'waiver'") with *Kiraly v. FBI,* 728 F.2d 273, 277-78 (6th Cir. 1984) (court distinguished tort recovery right for invasion of privacy from FOIA disclosure exemption, holding latter does not lapse upon death).
66. See, for example, *Cox Broadcasting Corp. v. Cohn,* 420 U.S. 469 (1975) (parent alleged that his right to privacy was invaded by identification of daughter as victim of rape-murder); *Corliss v. E. W. Walker Co.,* 57 F. 434 (C.C.D. Mass. 1893) *injunction dissolved,* 64 F. 280 (C.C.D. Mass. 1894) (plaintiff's alleged publication of biography and picture of dead husband and father constituted injury to their feelings).

67. "International Council of Archives at PAC," *ACA Bulletin* 10 (2) (November 1985), n.p.

The Administration of Access to Personal Information Held in Public Archives

Common Problems and Practices

As more and more researchers demand access to records containing personal information of varying degrees of sensitivity, archivists are faced with uneasy questions concerning the conditions, if any, under which access to all or some of these records is permissible. Taken together with changing public attitudes concerning the state's and the citizen's rights to personal information, changing trends in historical research and the ensuing pressure for more access to personal information held in government archives have forced archivists to reassess their traditional role as mediator in negotiating access and privacy rights. How do archivists negotiate access to records containing personal information when they are faced with recordkeeping environments that are statutorily confusing, contradictory, and occasionally incoherent with respect to their confidentiality?

In "Privacy Legislation: Implications for Archives," Judith Rowe suggests that "archivists are uniquely qualified to play the role of 'honest broker' between today's citizens and tomorrow's researchers."[1] A 1982 survey of fifty state archives, conducted by Alice Robbin, on the public policy issues of privacy and access to restricted records for social research demonstrates, however, that many archivists are ill-prepared to assume such a role[2] when records containing sensitive personal information are involved. Robbin surveyed the archivists' level of knowledge about state privacy, confidentiality, and open records laws and provisions for research access to confidential health and social services records, as well as the state archives' relationship with the creating agency. She found that, of the forty-seven state archives that responded to the questionnaire, thirty-four percent administered Health and Social Services (HSS) records and another six percent administered other types of confidential case records (e.g., inmate case files); yet archival policies and practices regarding access to confidential records were not well developed and archivists were not well informed about confidentiality and access statutes.

Although a prior review of privacy, confidentiality, and open records laws on access to confidential HSS records "revealed varying degrees of inconsistency, ambiguity, and conflict in the fifty state codes,"[3] almost three-quarters of the respondents said there were no conflicting state laws on disseminating or limiting access to HSS records administered by the archives. Nor were archivists well informed about either omnibus or special provisions to permit research or statistical use of confidential records. Forty-seven percent of the responses to the question, "Do any of these [HSS] statutes include a special provision for research access?" were incorrect, "with the archivists unable to identify correctly even one statute." [4]

Archivists were also asked about changes in the accessioning of and access to confidential records in response to recent laws. Thirty-three percent of the respondents indicated that changes had been made in the archives' access policies and procedures; leaving responsibility for access to the originating agency (unless there was an interagency agreement) was the change most frequently cited. The respondents' answers to questions concerning the archives' relationship with the originating agency further revealed that, on the whole, "[t]he originating agency usually played a decisive role in determining access; the archives had only a modest influence on such decisions."[5]

According to Robbin, the archivists' reluctance to make decisions on access was not attributable to either uncertainty or ambivalence about reconciling the competing values of privacy and access; seventy-seven percent of the respondents indicated they felt no ambivalence in balancing the two values.[6] Rather, the most frequent difficulty archivists encountered in determining access occurred:

> when the institutional or legal structure did not provide adequate cues. This occurred when the law did not close specific records and the archives and the agency disagreed about the conditions for release, when it was unclear whether the information was actually confidential and it could be harmful to families if released, or when confidentiality conflicted with appraisal requirements. [7]

Robbin's findings reinforced a similar conclusion reached by Margaret Hedstrom a couple of years earlier, that the clear lack of standards and mechanisms for reconciling the competing interests of privacy and access within government bureaucracies had made archivists:

> reluctant to become involved in determining how access to personal information will be regulated. ... By viewing their role as ambiguous, archivists have been reluctant to intervene on the side of either the individual citizen, who seeks increased protection of personal privacy, or the researcher who desires access to restricted information.[8]

Their reluctance is hardly surprising, given that legal requirements governing the management of and access to certain classes of records containing personal information are both unclear and confused and that technical and administrative procedures for providing legitimate access to elements of information contained in such records without compromising individual privacy and confidentiality do not appear to be well-developed or understood.

The lack of consistent or comprehensive provisions for confidentiality in government agencies is well documented in the report of the U.S. Privacy Protection Study Commission. In 1977, the Commission reviewed the statutory constraints on the use or disclosure of information about clients in a number of federally assisted welfare programs, including Medicaid, Food Stamps, Aid to Families with Dependent Children (AFDC), and Social Services (Title XX). It found that although federal statutes and regulations required the inclusion of confidentiality provisions in state plans for carrying out AFDC, Medicaid, and Title XX Social Services programs, the specific requirements differed from one program to the next. The laws governing other federally assisted programs, for example, Maternal and Child Health Services, did not include any confidentiality provision, and the policies of still others were inconsistent with those of the major programs.[9] The same lack of consistency typifies the administration of access to confidential records held by government agencies in Canada. In many jurisdictions, the same kinds of personal information are given inconsistent protection in different contexts. Before Ontario passed its Freedom of Information and Privacy Act in 1987, there was little uniformity in the statutory protection of personal information; for example, the Health Insurance Act, the Cancer Act, and the Workmen's Compensation Act all contained provisions to preserve the confidentiality of medical records. The Family Benefits Act, however, under which a great deal of both medical and financial information about individuals was collected by government agencies, contained no provisions for confidentiality.[10]

Records maintained in electronic systems exacerbate the problems. Policies and practices regarding the confidentiality of such records "often are arbitrary and vary among agencies," according to Margaret Hedstrom. "In some cases, access is denied to information that is neither statutorily nor administratively defined as confidential, merely because the records are in electronic form. In other cases, hard copy source documents may be defined explicitly as confidential by statute, yet access to the same information in electronic form may not be restricted."[11]

Another barrier archivists commonly encounter when they attempt to negotiate access to confidential records is the sheer number of statutes that may or may not apply to certain types of confidential records. The statutory withholding exemption or "pass-through" provision in the U. S. Freedom of Information Act,[12] for example, requires the withholding of information specifically exempted by a statute other than the FOIA.[13] In some states, such as Michigan, as many as twenty exemptions fall within the scope of the provision; in other states, such as Wisconsin, no exemptions are specified.[14] Gary Peterson and Trudy Huskamp Peterson suggest that the statutory withholding exemption

> is the most burdensome provision to administer for it assumes total knowledge of relevant statutes that may be found anywhere in the law codes. A 1984 survey of federal statutes found agencies using 135 laws with specific restrictions (for example, the restriction of raw census information for 72 years). States have an even greater problem. In addition to worrying about the federal laws that might apply through the state's own pass-through provision, there are state statutes that close off access to adoption records, to state income tax return information, to identities of state welfare recipients, and a host of others.[15]

A statutory withholding provision is also contained in the Canadian Access to Information Act, which requires the government to refuse to disclose records containing information, the disclosure of which is restricted pursuant to any statutory provision set out in Schedule II of the Act.[16] There are forty statutes with approximately fifty provisions in Schedule II, relating to income tax information, family allowance payments, labor union returns and raw census information. Although disclosure is prohibited absolutely under the Access Act, almost all the Schedule II statutes permit some limited disclosure, and more than half permit disclosure to the public. During the active life of the records that fall within these statutes, discretion to disclose is left to the Minister or other official within the affected agencies. Once the records are transferred to archival custody, it is not clear whether their exempt status changes.

Although most jurisdictions below the federal level in both the United States and Canada have some form of freedom of information law, only ten American states and three Canadian provinces have enacted comprehensive data protection legislation. In the absence of such legislation, state and provincial records laws frequently fail to distinguish between confidential and nonconfidential records; where confidentiality provisions are statutorily defined, there are often conflicting exemptions, particularly where responsibility for administering programs is shared between different government jurisdictions.[17]

Even in jurisdictions where access to information of a confidential nature is defined and limited, existing legislation frequently fails to clarify the conditions of use for records transferred to government archives.[18] Policies regarding the treatment of inactive files appear to have received little attention from government agencies and vary greatly by program and locale. In an American study of archival practices relating to the acquisition of public welfare case records, R. Joseph Anderson cited the archives' lack of legal authority over inactive case files as one of the primary impediments to state archives' accessioning public welfare case records. According to Anderson,

> the difficulties involved stem from the absence of statutory provisions for closed welfare records. Federal regulations specify that a single state agency must exercise control over active welfare files, but do not assign re-

sponsibility for closed files. Most state statutes similarly ignore inactive case files which creates enormous uncertainty for archivists attempting to administer access.[19]

A number of states have adopted legislation providing for the release of restricted records after a designated period or have passed separate statutes that provide for access for research purposes as well as administrative purposes. Nevertheless, access legislation and legislation by special statute, for example, statutes governing mental health records, vary a great deal, as Roland Baumann, in his survey of fourteen state programs for administering access to confidential records, discovered. "In some instances, legislation clearly provides that the conditions of use are the same in the agency and the archives. In other states, this provision is not incorporated or fully spelled out even though legal ownership resides with the originating agency."[20] Nor is the coverage of access laws consistent across jurisdictions; access laws "may or may not cover legislative, judicial and gubernatorial records and may not cover the records of the political subdivisions such as municipalities and counties."[21]

Faced with the kinds of recordkeeping environments described above, it is hardly surprising that government archivists typically address the problem of administering access to records containing confidential personal information by ceding responsibility to the record creating agency. While understandable, such a position is, nevertheless, untenable, given the archival profession's mission "to ensure the identification, preservation, and use of records of enduring value."[22] To carry out that mission, archivists need to have access to confidential records in order to appraise them; and, they need to develop procedures for transferring the records to archival custody and administering access to them.

Many archivists working in electronic divisions of government archives and in social science data archives[23] have concluded that the most appropriate means of mediating the competing interests of access and privacy is to simply reduce direct research access to personal information. Given the power of computers to manipulate data elements in individually identifiable records, they reason, the only ethical and practical way to resolve the privacy dilemma is to treat all personal information contained in records as confidential and to release files only when individuals cannot be identified.[24] The repository maintains two data files, one containing the raw data and the other containing the data in a public use or disclosure-free format. Personal information is processed so that the specific individuals to whom it relates cannot be identified and thus the information can be released for general research use.

Although anonymization procedures are not feasible as a means of administering access to large quantities of records maintained in manual systems where identifiers must be removed or blocked out by hand,[25] they are an effective means of administering access to electronic records containing personal information. There are, primarily, two approaches which can be taken with respect to data anonymization. The first is to remove all personally identifiable information from the file. In her examination of the technical procedures for protecting the confidentiality of electronic records, Margaret Hedstrom observes that, "in most studies, personal identifiers serve merely as an accounting device and they can be replaced with a set of case numbers unique to the research project without reducing the value of the records."[26] Nevertheless, there are small but significant categories of research for which personal identifiers are considered essential. In longitudinal research, which tracks an individual or group of individuals over time, personal identifiers are necessary to enable researchers to study characteristics of a study group at several points in time. Similarly, correlational research, which establishes relationships between characteristics of individuals, usually requires the linking of personal information held in separate records systems.

One means of addressing the need for individual identifiers without compromising individual privacy is through a link file strategy. Margaret Hedstrom explains the procedure thus:

> ... the computer is instructed to delete all personal identifiers and to assign a unique identification number to each case in a public use version of the file. The computer creates a second file that contains the personal identifiers and the unique identification number for each case. Using this procedure, the researcher can return to the archives for assistance in linking data from one file with additional records without ever ascertaining the identity of individuals in the restricted data file.[27]

Variations on the link file strategy include insulated file systems for settings in which information from different sources must be linked and brokerage systems, which refer to the maintenance of a link file by an unrelated third party whose function is to keep the identity of the record subject anonymous to the record user. [28]

Even if personal identifiers are deleted, however, the possibility of deductive or statistical disclosure may remain. According to Hedstrom, "in some data sets, cases are so unique that they can be identified on the basis of their attributes alone. For example, a data set on the characteristics of the population of a small town, including occupations, would permit identification of the doctor, the dentist, the hairdresser, the butcher, etc."[29] The possibility of deductive disclosure increases with the availability of other sources of information about the group under study.

The second approach to anonymizing data, one that avoids some of the pitfalls of the first, is to aggregate the information contained in one or more variables in such a way as to eliminate the identifying characteristics by submerging them in successively broader categories of information. Various data can be suppressed and classifications can be collapsed to limit the detail of small samples and prevent the disclosure of individual identities by way of cross classification.

A substantial body of literature has been developed by government census bureaus and social science data archives which describes a variety of methods for anonymizing data and for ensuring that users of aggregated data cannot identify record subjects.[30] In his RAMP study of the issues associated with the archival administration of electronic records, Harold Naugler suggests that, "where possible, aggregation should be the desired means to anonymize a data file," because:

> Removing information from a file always represents an absolute information loss. Whatever amount of knowledge about the study group was contained in a deleted variable is completely unavailable to the researcher, and since the information collected for inclusion in a data file generally has a specific, and important purpose, its elimination affects the usefulness of the other data. Similarly, aggregation represents information loss but usually not as completely as does deletion. The effect of aggregation is to reduce the degree of specificity of the data. As a variable is successively aggregated, fewer research questions can be addressed and fewer problems can be analyzed. [31]

Criticisms of microaggregation have focused precisely on this last point. Social science historian Allan Bogue objects to the aggregation of microlevel data on the grounds that, "once the basic individual unit of data is gone and we are forced to depend upon an agency aggregative summary, or one done by an earlier scholar, we can never again recapture the individual characteristics for certain."[32]

The growth in demographic studies has created an increasing demand for quantifiable microlevel data in electronic form, since the informational value of electronic records is proportional to their level of aggregation. According to Charles Dollar:

> summary information at the county level is more valuable than summary information at the state level. But this county level information is less valuable than information on individual persons, places or things because summarized data cannot be disaggregated. In contrast, one can always summarize or aggregate the individual

information to the desired summary level. Consequently, individual data or unaggregated microlevel information has the greatest potential for statistical manipulation.[33]

In a 1978 brief to the federal government, the Canadian Association of University Teachers (CAUT) indicated that both the CAUT and the Canadian Historical Association share the view that: "Certain kinds of research necessitate access to microdata at an identifiable individual level.... The publication of aggregated information from census and other surveys is not sufficient as it cannot take into consideration all of the concerns of scholars."[34]

Anonymization procedures such as those described above have the advantage of reducing the researchers' need to access and maintain individually identifiable records and permitting researchers access to information when data protection laws or regulation might otherwise prevent it. Nevertheless, they are limited in a number of ways. Procedures used to create disclosure-free versions of restricted data files often are expensive to design and implement, and they require technical skills that at present are not common to archivists. From the researcher's point of view, any of the methods described above could reduce the usefulness of data for some types of statistical analysis. Some prevent the effective appraisal of the validity of samples or the validity of the records on which research is based; others impede linkage with independent sources of information, thereby making validation studies difficult to perform. Anonymizing or aggregating data involves "the suppression and ultimate loss" of raw or microlevel data that scholars want "preserved in usable and accessible form"[35] Given the consensus of the research community that access to individually identifiable information is necessary for certain kinds of studies, and the limited scope of application for anonymization procedures, it is doubtful they will ever constitute the sole means by which archivists administer access to confidential personal information.

Perhaps the commonest method of providing research access to individually identifiable records is through special clearance procedures which impose certain requirements on the users of such records before access is granted. Screening procedures based either on the credentials of the researcher and/or on the perceived legitimacy of the research project have been used by some archives as a method of determining whether access to records containing sensitive personal information will be granted. In the United States, several state archives have set as a condition of access to confidential government case files "the demonstration of legitimate purpose by the researcher," which the archivist ascertains through initial screening interviews and consultations with the source agency.[36] Researchers seeking access to sensitive personal information held by the U.S National Archives and Records Administration (NARA) are required to submit a proposal that includes, in addition to a description of the project itself, their institutional affiliation, a list of published research, and references.[37] *Bona fide* researcher credentials are also one of the prerequisites for access to restricted records held in the Archives of Ontario.

Screening procedures also figure in the contractual agreements that government archivists, particularly in the United States, are increasingly initiating with record-creating agencies and researchers to negotiate access to confidential personal information. Many such agreements have been developed at the state level and do not appear, for the most part, to be either authorized or required by law. According to Roland Baumann, "such agreements are utilized when no clear legal provisions govern the transfer of confidential records from an agency to the state archives, or when no written research guidelines are in place to regulate access to records that are presumably restricted and already in the custody of the state archives."[38]

The model for this type of contractual agreement was first outlined in a 1974 article by Virginia Stewart in the *American Archivist*. In that article, she articulated the need for archival repositories to develop policy "covering acquisition, custody, and access to case records" from a theoretical and legal perspective,[39] and she described the policy on access that the Manuscript Section of the University of Illinois Library had developed in order to deal with confidential public-welfare case files. The policy incorporated a number of conditions for access, requiring that researchers: complete an application outlining their research proposal; agree in writing to maintain the confidentiality of the records; allow their research notes and any publication(s) arising from the research to be reviewed; and agree to "hold harmless and indemnify" the archives against any loss or damage arising out of use of the records.[40] A similar arrangement was adopted by the Michigan State Archives in 1978 to acquire and administer access to mental health records from a state hospital for the criminally insane. Michigan's interagency contract operates at the level of the source agency as well as the researcher; all research requests approved by the archives are forwarded to the Department of Mental Health for final review and approval.[41] Under the terms of the Michigan agreement, researchers are obliged to accept conditions of access almost identical to those developed by Virginia Stewart.[42]

Because contractual agreements of the type described above have no legislative basis, their comprehensiveness and their effectiveness are constrained by their dependence on the originating agency's cooperation in delegating authority in this area to the state archives. Roland Baumann reports that, in New York and Wisconsin, attempts to negotiate specific agreements with record-creating agencies "have yielded 'mixed results.' "[43] A more comprehensive system of contracted access to records containing sensitive personal information has been developed at the federal level in the United States and Canada. Both the U.S. National Archives and Records Administration (NARA) and the National Archives of Canada have drafted a set of administrative procedures that permit researchers limited access to personal information implicating significant privacy values, under specified conditions.

At the same time, NARA decided to place itself within the scope of the FOIA for the purpose of administering access to the records in its custody, it also requested, and received, from Congress a virtual exemption from the provisions of the Privacy Act,[44] which prohibits the disclosure of personal records (within a system of records) for research or statistical purposes in individually identifiable form. In requesting the exemption, NARA contended (among other things) that sufficient restrictions, imposed by statute, the transferring agency, and NARA itself, already existed to protect individual privacy.[45]

The restrictions imposed by NARA are outlined in the U.S. Code of Federal Regulations.[46] Under the regulations, NARA restricts from access records which would clearly invade the privacy of an individual, which are defined as:

> records containing information about a living individual which reveals details of a highly personal nature that the individual could reasonably assert a claim to withhold from the public to avoid a clearly unwarranted invasion of privacy, including but not limited to information about the physical or mental health or the medical or psychiatric care or treatment of the individual and that—(1) contain personal information not known to have been previously made public, and (2) relate to events less than 75 years old.[47]

It may, however, authorize access to such records for the purpose of statistical or quantitative research to "qualified persons doing biomedical research" under prescribed conditions. Researchers are required to submit their research proposal to NARA's review committee, outlining, in addition to their research credentials, the nature of the research to be conducted and any plans for the publication or presentation of the research findings; the methodology that will be applied; a listing of the records to be used; and an indication of the physical and technical safeguards that the researcher will use to prevent any unauthorized use or disclosure of the records.

The review committee will examine the research proposal to determine, for example, whether the information is so sensitive to preclude even quantitative research; the proposed methodology will permit the projected research results without revealing personally identifying information; the requesters are *bona fide* biomedical researchers with experience; and whether the proposed safeguards will adequately protect the information. If the project is approved, the researchers and all others associated with the project who have access to personally identifiable information must agree in writing to maintain the confidentiality of the information and to abide by the conditions of access imposed by NARA, which, depending on the nature of the project, may include that records be used only for the purpose of the approved research project; that any individually identifiable information in the researcher's notes or in authorized copies of the records be rendered anonymous by the researcher at the earliest possible time consistent with the purpose of the project; that final research products be provided to NARA prior to publication or presentation, to ensure that there is no possible identification of individuals; and that all research notes containing individually identifiable information and/or copies of individually identifiable records be destroyed or returned to NARA once the project is completed.

Researchers who fail to comply with the conditions of access are subject to a variety of penalties including the revoking of research privileges and, possibly, notification of the researcher's institution, referees, and funding agencies who supported the project, as well as relevant professional organizations. Legal steps may also be taken to prevent any further disclosure of the information.

An analogous system of contracted access has been developed by the National Archives of Canada to permit research access to records containing personal information under section 8(2)(j) of the Canadian Privacy Act, which permits personal information under the control of any government institution, including the National Archives, to be disclosed for research purposes under specified conditions.[48] According to the National Archives' guidelines for disclosure of personal information, the purpose of this provision is to provide an avenue for research and statistical analysis involving personal information, especially in medicine and the social sciences, while making researchers formally accountable for the protection of individual privacy when they are allowed access to such information.[49]

The provision permits access to extensive series of records that contain personal information and that are systematically organized or retrieved by the name of an individual or by an identifying number, symbol, or other particular assigned to an individual. Examples of records that fall into this category are case files such as Unemployment Insurance Commission benefit claims files, civil service personnel records, and pilots' files.[50]

The conditions under which personal information may be disclosed are similar to those established in the NARA regulations.[51] Researchers are required to submit their research proposal to a review committee which will review it, taking into account any statutory prohibitions on access, the sensitivity of the information relative to its contents and currency, and the record subjects' expectations of confidentiality. The committee will also evaluate the project's methodology, to determine whether the projected research results can be achieved without the disclosure of individually identifiable information.

Once the proposal is approved, researchers are required to agree in writing that no subsequent disclosure of the information will be made in a form that could identify the individual(s) to whom it relates; to comply with conditions on access and use that may include the anonymization of personal information at the earliest possible time; to append to the approval a list of the data linkages which have been sanctioned; and, to agree not to form other data linkages without the written authorization of the National Archives.

Conceptually, the use of screening procedures to determine whether or not access to records containing sensitive personal information is permissible and the use of contractual agreements to ensure that the confidentiality of such information is respected by researchers offer an appropriate and necessary means of negotiating access to such records. Their symbolic effect in sensitizing the research community to the need to protect personal privacy cannot be underestimated. Nonetheless, the practical application of these procedures and, specifically, the criteria for disclosure established by them are a less than satisfactory means of balancing equitably the interests of researchers against the privacy interests of record subjects.

A significant drawback to the screening of researchers and/or vetting of research notes or results generally is that they require archivists to intercede in the research process in a manner many might find objectionable. Although such practices are intended only to ensure that the confidentiality of sensitive information is respected by researchers, they are rightly viewed with skepticism by many archivists because they set up the archivist as the final arbiter of what studies may be published. Jean Tener, for example, notes that, "too much discretionary power presents the danger that the archivist will become policeman and censor."[52]

Screening procedures that attempt to limit access to so-called *bona fide* researchers (i.e., those possessing academic research credentials) or "legitimate" research projects also imply that a clear-cut and defensible distinction may be drawn between serious and nonserious research and that the archivist has a right to make judgments as to who can use the information under the archives' control, as well as how that information can be used. Tener argues persuasively that access should be regarded:

> as something which cannot be divided into open categories for "scholars" and closed categories for "sensational writers," or available to those with a "genuine" interest and unavailable to those who lack an appropriate "appreciation." Access should be indivisible.[53]

The traditional notion of "legitimate" research as the exclusive domain of the scholar has not gone unchallenged. In a court decision in the Netherlands relating to a refusal to grant access to archives to a journalist, for example, the judge decided in favor of the journalist, concluding that, "the dividing line between scientific research and nonscientific research cannot be determined solely by the nature of the publication for which the result of this research is intended."[54]

Public repositories contain public property, and because they are supported by taxes, they must be maintained in the service of all citizens. Michel Duchein maintains that

> limitations on access to the public archives for the benefit of certain categories of research, hence of researchers, must be considered contrary not only to the principle of the freedom of information but also that of the equality of all before the law. Universities and historians should not make up a privileged category of citizens for access to documentation, which is the property of all.[55]

Moreover, the application of an intellectual means test for access to records containing personal information is an elitist practice that is incompatible with the democratic spirit of archival principles that have been developed since 1945. The ICA draft law on production and right of access encourages access without distinction made between users,[56] and the Society of American Archivists' 1973 statement on *Standards for Access to Research Materials* advocates that repositories "not grant privileged or exclusive use of materials to any person or persons."[57]

Another limitation of contractual agreements, particularly the state-administered ones, is their heavy reliance on researchers' voluntary self-regulation to ensure the protection of record subjects' privacy during the research project and for an indefinite period thereafter. Although most of the archives that use contractual agreements reserve the right to review research findings, there is little provision for systematic continuing review of research projects that have been approved, to ensure that the procedural and technical safeguards outlined in the research proposal are in place and are functioning effectively. The archives' responsibility for this type of continuing review is not clearly defined in any of the agreements, an omission that is not only inconsistent with the custodial responsibility archivists assume for the records in their care but also potentially risky, particularly when extremely sensitive information is involved. The risk has prompted at least one critic to suggest that in cases involving the use of records implicating significant privacy values, archivists should take the view that, "if the data is too sensitive to allow the researcher to use it in the way he/she sees fit, then it is really too sensitive to be seen in the first place."[58]

The threat of legal and financial penalties for the violation of access conditions built into the contractual agreements carries a certain symbolic value as a deterrent against abuse. Nevertheless, enforced promises of confidentiality and the threat of penalties are no guarantee that personal information will not be further disclosed by researchers, either deliberately or inadvertently; penalties imposed after the damage has been done remain remedies of despair, as common law experience attests. Nor will such measures protect personal information against compulsory disclosure in the event a researcher's notes are subpoenaed. Current legal standards are based on the assumption that the obligation to facilitate accurate and informed decisions in judicial and administrative proceedings should take precedence over any promises of confidentiality or possible effects upon research or statistical activities. Researchers do not enjoy the same testimonial privilege accorded to applied professionals such as doctors or lawyers, and records that enjoy statutory protection from compulsory process are extremely limited.[59] Prosecutors, grand juries, legislative bodies, civil litigants, and administrative agencies all can use their subpoena powers to compel disclosure of confidential research information.

The subpoenaing of research information has been most evident when social research into illegal or stigmatized behavior is involved. A social research experiment involving welfare clients in New Jersey, for example, provoked attempts by a grand jury, at least two welfare departments, the General Accounting Office, and the Senate Finance Committee to secure confidential data compiled during the experiment, sometimes by subpoena, in order to track down fraudulent welfare recipients.[60] In another incident, three scholars were subpoenaed because of their possible knowledge concerning the private publication of the Pentagon Papers. In all three cases, the courts denied the social scientists the right to withhold information acquired with a promise of confidentiality.[61]

The examples suggest that the threat of subpoena is real and that researchers have no general basis for protection that will be recognized by the courts. With respect to socio-historical uses of personal information, the danger of subpoena may present itself, for example, when data linkages are made using personal information collected by different government agencies from different jurisdictions. If the profile that results from the combination of personal information from different sources reveals information of interest to an administrative or judicial body, it could be subpoenaed and used as the basis for a decision adversely affecting an individual who happens to be included in the group under study. The fact that, according to some contractual agreements, the archives is indemnified and therefore cannot be held accountable as a general publisher[62] offers small consolation to the individual whose privacy is violated or to the archives whose reputation will certainly suffer in the event a breach of confidentiality does occur.

From the broader social perspective of privacy concerns, it is equally clear that a system of paternalistic checks and balances fails to address fully the substantive issue at the heart of the defense of personal privacy, which is the right of the individual to a reasonable degree of secrecy and anonymity. Restricting access to so-called "serious" researchers or research, or placing conditions on use, does not dispel the ethical ambiguity surrounding the disclosure of personal information to third parties without the consent of the individual concerned. That the member-

The Administration of Access

ship of the review boards established by the NARA and the National Archives of Canada to decide on access requests involving sensitive personal information fails to include anyone who might speak more directly on behalf of record subjects only exacerbates the ambiguity.[63]

Historians argue that denying researchers access to records containing personal information, even sensitive information, is a violation of the principle of freedom of inquiry, the scholar's right to pursue and to communicate knowledge in the interest of a greater societal good. Allan Bogue, for example, "see[s] no great threat in full disclosure of an individual's transactions with government."[64] Arguing that data under extreme confidentiality restrictions may be as useless as data destroyed, Bogue urges archivists not to abet or contribute to what he terms the "hysteria over privacy."[65] Instead, he argues:

> we must prevent restrictions in mindless ways or the result will be the destruction of data of historical consequence or restricted access for ridiculously long periods of time. The position that we should close records to protect individuals is much less in the interests of the historical researcher and the public than is the principle that there should be appropriate penalties for the misuse of information derived from personal records . . .[66]

While the principle Bogue advocates certainly serves the interests of historians (since its application would increase research access), its public interest is less clear, since it fails to accommodate the public's interest in (and right to) privacy, which requires protective measures before, as well as after, the fact of disclosure. The argument against restrictions is understandable, even defensible from the historians' perspective, because the research community to which they belong, and are answerable, shares a common vision predicated on the primary value of research. Government archivists, however, answer to multiple constituencies that include, in addition to the research community, the sponsoring agency and the public at large. The position they adopt with respect to privacy and access rights must, in consequence, reflect a more equitable balance between the competing values.

Most of the state archivists surveyed by Alice Robbin indicated that they did not experience any dilemma when balancing the competing values of privacy and access. According to Robbin, "either the right to privacy was deemed the principal value, or the right to access for the benefits that research could bring to society outweighed the privacy right."[67] Despite the apparent lack of ambivalence, however, this finding suggests that, at least among the archivists surveyed, there is not a clear consensus on which value—access or privacy—ought to be paramount. Does freedom of inquiry possess a moral value that is equal to, or which overrides, individual rights to privacy? Or should privacy be considered the overriding value when the two interests conflict?

On the whole, although archivists do not dispute the significance of privacy interests, they have been more inclined to publicly promote the virtues of access. The Association of Canadian Archivists, for example, has warned that large-scale closures of personal records:

> would cause a serious deterioration of publications on the development of Canadian society. For example, the production of scholarly works currently being written on the settlement of the West, the depression, World War II, immigration and ethnic communities, which rely heavily on correspondence from and concerning individuals would be seriously curtailed and the ability to increase our knowledge in understanding our Canadian culture would be seriously impaired.[68]

When it drafted its model archives law in 1972 which opened records containing personal information after 50 years, the International Council on Archives recognized the conflict of values between access and privacy, but it concluded that "the principle of free access . . . should no longer have to be sacrificed every time it clashes . . . with the privacy of individuals."[69] But is such a position morally defensible? To answer that question, we need to examine more closely the ethical issues underlying the disclosure of personal information for research purposes.

Notes

1. Judith Rowe, "Privacy Legislation: Implications for Archives," *Archivists and Machine-Readable Records* (see chapt. 2, n.2), 194.

2. For more detailed survey results, see Alice Robbin, "State Archives and Issues of Personal Privacy: Policies and Practices," *American Archivist* 49 (Spring 1986): 163-75.

3. Ibid., 167.
4. Ibid., 167-68.
5. Ibid., 168.
6. Ibid., 172.
7. Ibid., 173.

8. Margaret L. Hedstrom, "Computers, Privacy, and Research Access to Confidential Information," *Midwestern Archivist* 6 (1) (1981): 6.

9. For example, federal policies on disclosure of alcohol and drug abuse treatment records differed from those applicable to records maintained under the Title XX program, which also funds alcohol and drug abuse treatment services, creating confusion as to which rules apply to records maintained under both Title XX and other federal government funding programs. See Privacy Protection Study Commission, *Personal Privacy in an Information Society* (see chapt. 2, n.38), 448-54.

10. The confusing and sometimes contradictory recordkeeping policies and practices of the Ontario Ministry of Community and Social Services have been exhaustively documented in Michael Brown, Brenda Billingsley, and Rebecca Shamai, *Privacy and Personal Data Protection: A Report on Personal Record-Keeping by the Ministries and Agencies of the Ontario Government* (Commission on Freedom of Information and Individual Privacy, 1980), 228-338.

11. Hedstrom, "Computers, Privacy, and Research Access," 9.

12. 5 U.S.C., 552(b) (3).

13. The U. S. Privacy Act does not fall within the meaning of (b) (3). See 5 U.S.C., 552a (q) (2).

14. Gary M. Peterson and Trudy Huskamp Peterson, *Archives and Manuscripts: Law* (Chicago: Society of American Archivists, 1985), 46.

15. Ibid., 48-49.

16. *Access to Information Act,* S.C. 1980-81-82-83, c.111, s.24.

17. The Petersons point out that the 1980 adoption of the Uniform Information Practices Code by the National Conference on Commissioners on Uniform State Laws may increase the uniformity of state freedom of information and privacy laws in the United States. For a summary of the Code, see Peterson and Peterson, *Archives and Manuscripts: Law,* 59.

18. Roland Baumann, "Administration of Access to Confidential Records" (see chapt. 4, n.44), 355.

19. Anderson, "Public Welfare Case Records" (see chapt. 4, n.44), 177. See also Baumann, "Administration of Access to Confidential Records," 355.

20. Baumann, "Administration of Access to Confidential Records," 357.

21. Ibid., 355.

22. *Planning for the Archival Profession: A Report of the SAA Task Force on Goals and Priorities* (Chicago: Society of American Archivists, 1986), vi.

23. Social science data archives receive data from a variety of sources with the specific objective of organizing these data into electronic form for purposes of subsequent redissemination and utilization in a variety of research settings. See Joseph Steinberg, "Social Research Use of Archival Records: Procedural Solutions to Privacy Problems," *Solutions to Ethical and Legal Problems in Social Research,* ed. Robert F. Boruch and Joe S. Cecil (New York: Academic Press, 1983), 249-62.

24. See, for example, Charles M. Dollar, "Machine-Readable Records of the Federal Government and the National Archives," *Archivists and Machine-Readable Records,* 85; and Harold Naugler, "The Machine-Readable Archives Program of the Public Archives of Canada," *Archivists and Machine-Readable Records,* 76.

25. The Public Archives of Canada and the University of Saskatchewan have developed a procedure in which sensitive information is removed from microfilmed legal records by covering certain frames on the film with light sensitive tape prior to producing duplicate copies of the records. See James M. Whalen, "The Application of Solicitor-Client Privilege to Government Records," *Archivaria* 18 (Summer 1984): 148.

26. Hedstrom, "Computers, Privacy, and Research Access," 13.

27. Ibid., 14.

28. See, for example, Robert F. Boruch and Joe S. Cecil, *Assuring the Confidentiality of Social Science Research Data* (Philadelphia, Penna.: University of Pennsylvania Press, 1979), 108-12.

29. Hedstrom, "Computers, Privacy, and Research Access," 14-15.

30. See, for example, Boruch and Cecil, eds., *Solutions to Ethical and Legal Problems in Social Research;* Boruch and Cecil, *Assuring the Confidentiality of Social Research Data;* David H. Flaherty, *Privacy and Government Data Banks: An International Perspective* (London: Mansell Publishing, 1979).

31. Harold Naugler, *The Archival Appraisal of Machine-Readable Records: A RAMP Study with Guidelines* (Paris: Unesco, 1984), 86.

32. Allen Bogue, "Historical Research and State Archival Data," *Archivists and Machine-Readable Records,* 26.

33. Charles M. Dollar, "Machine-Readable Records of the Federal Government and the National Archives," *Archivists and Machine-Readable Records,* 83.

34. "Freedom of Information: A Brief submitted to the Government of Canada by the Canadian Association of University Teachers," 1978, 3.

35. In Tener, "Accessibility and Archives" (see chapt. 2, n.19), 29.

36. Anderson, "Public Welfare Case Records," 174.

37. 36 CFR ch. XII (7-1-88 Edition), 1256.16(a).

38. Baumann, "Administration of Access to Confidential Records," 360.

39. Stewart, "Problems of Confidentiality," (see chapt. 4, n.44), 396.

40. Ibid.

41. See Baumann, "Administration of Access to Confidential Records," 362.

42. Ibid., 363.

43. Ibid., 364.

44. NARA is still required to publish an annual notice of the systems of records in its holdings that contain personal information.

45. James E. O'Neill, "Federal Law and Access to Federal Records," *Access to the Papers of Recent Public Figures: The New Harmony Conference,* eds. Alonzo L. Hamby and Edward Wel-

don (Bloomington, Ind.: American Historical Association, Organization of American Historians, Society of American Archivists Committee on Historians and Archivists, 1977), 41.

46. 36 CFR Ch. XII (7-1-88 Edition), 1256.4.
47. 36 CFR Ch. XII (7-1-88 Edition), 1256.16(a).
48. The Archives of Ontario, which is also covered under access and privacy legislation, has a similar system of contracted access.
49. Public Archives of Canada, *Guidelines for the Disclosure of Personal Information*, 7.
50. Ibid.
51. Ibid., Appendix 3.
52. Tener, "Accessibility and Archives," 26.
53. Ibid.
54. Cited in Duchein, *Obstacles to the Access, Use and Transfer of Information* (see chapt. 2, n.35), 30.
55. Ibid., 28.
56. Tener, "Accessibility and Archives," 18.
57. Holbert, *Archives and Manuscripts: Reference and Access* (see chapt. 4, n.56), 9.
58. Helen Yoxall, "Privacy and Personal Papers," *Archives and Manuscripts* 12 (May 1984): 42.
59. Existing U. S. statutes that specifically protect research information on identifiable respondents against compulsory process are described in Robert F. Boruch, "Resolving Privacy Problems in Social Research," in *Ethical Issues in Social Science Research*, eds. Tom L. Beauchamp et al. (Baltimore, Md.: Johns Hopkins University Press, 1982), 302-08; and in Lois Alexander, "Proposed Legislation to Improve Statistical and Research Access to Federal Records," in *Solutions to Ethical and Legal Problems in Social Research*, eds. Boruch and Cecil, 273-98.
60. See D. N. Kershaw and J. C. Small, "Data Confidentiality and Privacy: Lessons from the New Jersey Negative Income Tax Experiment," *Public Policy* 20 (1972): 257-80.
61. The case is outlined in Paul Reynolds, *Ethical Dilemmas and Social Science Research* (San Francisco: Jossey Bass, 1979), 314. See also J. D. Carroll, "Confidentiality of Social Science Research and Data: The Popkin Case," *Political Science* 6 (3) (1973): 268-80; P. Nejelski and H. Peyser, "A Researcher's Shield Statute: Guarding Against the Compulsory Disclosure of Research Data," Appendix B to *Protecting Individual Privacy in Evaluation Research* (Washington, D. C.: National Academy of Sciences, 1975).

62. According to Virginia Stewart, in the absence of a written statement by researchers that they will "hold harmless and indemnify" the archives, "a repository furnishing material to a researcher may incur liability as 'general publisher' to lawsuits arising from published research." See Stewart, "Problems of Confidentiality," 390, n.11.

63. At NARA, the access review committee consists of the Deputy Archivist of the United States, the Assistant Archivist for the National Archives, and the director(s) of the NARA division(s) which has custody of the requested records. The committee may consult other persons inside and outside the Federal Government who are knowledgeable in the research field for assistance in evaluating a request. At the National Archives of Canada, the access review committee is chaired by the National Archivist and includes the Director General of the Archives Branch, the Departmental Access to Information Coordinator, the Chief of the Access Section, and may include an archivist familiar with the records requested and an outside assessor, who may be either from another federal agency or an academic.

64. Bogue, "Historical Research and State Archival Data," *Archivists and Machine-Readable Records*, 26.

65. Ibid., 27.

66. Bogue, "Data Dilemmas," *Social Science History*, 213-14.

67. Robbin, "State Archives and Issues of Personal Privacy," 175.

68. "Submission of the Association of Canadian Archivists to the Parliamentary Committee on Justice and Legal Affairs with Respect to Bill C-43," n.d., 12.

69. Quoted in Jean Tener, "Accessibility and Archives," 18.

Research Uses of Personal Information

Some Ethical Considerations

> Without respect for human dignity and forbearance before human frailty, there can be no privacy in the sense of either seclusion or protection against authority.
>
> Barrington Moore
> *Privacy*

Early in 1986, fifteen thousand Swedes who were born in 1953 discovered that their lives had been under a microscope since the day they were born as a result of a secret sociological study. Newspapers disclosed[1] that researchers at Stockholm University had been amassing computerized files on every person born in Stockholm in 1953 as part of a project called "Metropolit." There are approximately one hundred thousand computer registers containing information on individuals in Sweden. More than six hundred were set up by the government and cover everything from education, health, social problems, and absences from work, to taxes, rents, and military service. Using information supplied by virtually all public bodies, including confidential data from police and health authorities, the researchers put together encyclopedic files which included the subjects' school record, sexual problems, performance at work, family ties, income, and crimes. The purpose of the research, according to a member of the Metropolit project, was apparently "to see how things are for people in life." Carl-Gunnar Janson, a Sociology professor at Stockholm University and the leader of the Metropolit project, defended the research on the grounds that "it would be grotesque if those interviewed were able to rob me of material which I have been working with for more than 20 years. The idea that they can own the information about themselves is fantastic."

That same week, the Swedish Data Inspection Board, whose job is to protect Swedes against abuses of information held about them in government computers, reported that scientists at the Karolinska Institute had assembled a file on women who had legal abortions between 1966 and 1974; the Institute used the file in a study of the links between abortion and cancer. None of the women were told their names were on the Institute's computers. The two incidents are worth noting because they occurred in a country whose data protection laws are considered the most stringent in the world.

When Emile Durkheim published *The Elementary Forms of Religious Life*, he looked forward to the time when science would take over the subjects that religion and philosophy had traditionally sought to explain: nature, humankind, and society. Science, he proclaimed, would "set aside the veil with which mythological imagination had covered these subjects for them to appear as they really are."[2] The illusion that social transparency is achievable has driven research in the social sciences ever since. Many social benefits have derived from the pursuit of that illusion, but there have also been costs. The steady erosion of personal privacy is by no means the least of the costs.

The ethics of disclosing personal information for research and statistical purposes will be explored in this chapter within the general context of social research; and the more specific context of socio-historical research that requires government records containing personal information as a source of data. A distinguishing feature of this type of research is that the information was obtained from, or about, individuals on an earlier occasion and for a different purpose. Here, invasions of privacy occur to the extent that record subjects are unable to determine what information about themselves they will disclose and how that information will be disseminated; violations of confidentiality occur when information about a record subject is disseminated to audiences for whom it was not intended.[3] The question such research raises is whether customary moral restraints governing the disclosure of personal information should be overridden for the sake of academic inquiry.

The traditional rationale for research serves partly to answer, partly to deflect that question. Though fewer now believe in the possibility of attaining "true knowledge" than in Durkheim's time, most will argue that research may at least push back the boundaries of ignorance and felt chaos.[4] Freedom of academic (or scientific) inquiry in the pursuit of knowledge is a value typically expressed in its own right and in opposition to the regulation of research. The concern that constraints placed on research will hobble opportunities to produce new scientific ideas and stifle scientific innovation is the basis on which scholars have argued for the principle expressed as "the freedom to pursue and develop any issue that seems of intellectual significance, relying solely on the evaluation of other scientists to determine which new ideas will be accepted as useful after they have been fully developed and compared with data from research."[5] Scholarly researchers argue that, "a society which limits the academics' area of inquiry and expression is hurting itself by reducing its potential for knowledge."[6]

The tradition of the autonomy of the researcher is supported by theories concerning the process of scientific discovery and the conditions that are required to foster it. In *The Structure of Scientific Revolutions,* Thomas Kuhn introduced the notion that science advances by means of "paradigm shifts," in which the beliefs, values, and techniques shared by the members of a given scientific community are challenged by the discovery (or cumulative discoveries) of anomalies within the established framework of theory. According to Kuhn, the "failure of existing rules is the prelude to a search for new ones."[7] Old paradigms are not, however, easily surrendered. Paradigm shifts can only occur in a nutritive environment that allows for repeated trial and error, permits scientists the freedom to pursue hunches and undefined lines of inquiry without formalizing the hypotheses guiding their research, and encourages scientists to consider alternatives to established ideas.[8] To the extent that restrictions on research methodology would make some studies impossible to perform, some scholars argue, such restrictions "infringe the scientist's right to illuminate still mysterious regions of human understanding."[9]

Because scholarly research needs to be protected against censorship, blacklists, or limitations on the study of certain subjects, many researchers have been reluctant to accept regulation or control of any kind over research. John Robertson observes that some social scientists "question the very legitimacy of any government regulation of social research. In their view, scientists have a right to plan and conduct research as they see fit, subject only to judgments of their peers based on canons of scientific validity."[10] Arguments that favor researchers' autonomy assert that researchers should be free to decide what kinds of research they will perform and how they wish to conduct that research. According to this view, freedom of inquiry should be protected from outside interference unless there are strong reasons for overriding the presumption of freedom. Canadian historian Robert Craig Brown, for example, believes that:

> At bottom, the manic pursuit in government agencies and university administration for codes, guides, regulations and bureaucratic impediments is a disavowal of trust in the integrity of the researcher and his or her research.
>
> ... What is needed, Professor [Roger] Graham concluded in 1971, "is a reaffirmation of the principle that as far

as the world of scholarship is concerned, the public interest is served by protecting to the greatest possible extent the freedom of the scholar, provided that it is coupled with a sober sense of responsibility . . . to use that freedom, and with it the public funds that support him, judiciously and well."[11]

Regulations, guidelines, and other restrictions on research, however, may be less a disavowal of trust in the researcher than a prudent response to the changing environment in which research is conducted. As Sissela Bok makes clear, the desire to protect freedom of inquiry should not blind us to the fact that the words *freedom* and *inquiry* can be stretched far beyond freedom of thought:

> Their placid connotations can then help to ward off concern about what scientists do, and about limits to invasive . . . research. The concept of "inquiry" in science evokes the solitary seeker for knowledge. Freedom of such inquiry is freedom of limitless thought and unfettered speech. . . . [Yet the] solitary, reflective, almost passive connotations of "scientific inquiry" do not in fact correspond with many of the activities of today's scientists. These men and women are hardly solitary in their interaction with others. They are far from passive in their use of vast public funds . . .[12]

The obligation to advance knowledge is only one among a large number of social obligations that affect scholarly researchers, and these other obligations can easily impose alternative and conflicting imperatives.

Supporters of unrestrained research argue that knowledge is better than ignorance and that a scientific end justifies the means used to achieve it. Critics counter with the argument that scientific freedom is not an absolute right, but rather an institutional norm which must be weighed against other norms to find the balance most conducive to promoting social welfare.[13] It is useful to recall that during the Nuremberg trials, the international research community essentially endorsed the latter view when it rejected the grounds on which Nazi medical "research" was defended, those grounds being that, "the welfare of the species overr[ode] the welfare of the particular man."[14]

In seeking the balance most conducive to promoting social welfare, we need to bear in mind the distinction Christian Bay draws between a "social privilege" and a "right" and ask ourselves whether academic freedom should more properly be considered a social privilege rather than a right. According to Bay:

> "Right" refers to a protected freedom. "Human right" refers to a kind of freedom that can be, and therefore, must be, made available to and protected for all the people in a given society. A freedom that cannot be extended to all is an example of a "social privilege". . . . [and] in a free society a privilege must yield whenever it demonstrably becomes an obstacle to a fuller protection and expansion of human rights.[15]

The principle of academic freedom does not lend any special legitimacy to practices considered otherwise disrespectful of persons. However much we may value freedom of inquiry in the pursuit of knowledge, we must insist that a critical difference exists between the freedom to conduct research and the freedom to involve human subjects in research. The second freedom is considerably more limited than the first.

Given that the principle of academic freedom does not, in itself, adequately justify research that requires the use of personal information, defenses of potentially invasive social research frequently draw more specifically on the beneficial consequences deriving from research. According to this utilitarian argument, the professional obligation to advance human understanding is taken to include a positive moral duty to provide social benefits. The principle of beneficence is used to ascertain classes of actions that are morally permissible to achieve beneficial ends; ethical dilemmas are resolved by balancing the risk of harm to subjects against the potential benefits of research.

Is it appropriate, though, to justify social research in terms of the social benefits it promises to produce? The risk-benefit model is drawn from biomedical research in which specific improvements in health care delivery or cost reductions can be cited as important social benefits. It is not really possible to invoke comparable benefits in performing risk-benefit assessments in the social sciences, since considerable social research aims primarily at the acquisition of knowledge and only secondarily, if at all, at the beneficial applications which may result from that knowledge. As Herbert Kelman observes, "[t]he benefits to be derived from social research largely take the form of contributions to science and society; these contributions are not readily predictable or demonstrable—and in any case, they do not directly advance the well-being of the participants themselves."[16]

More significantly perhaps, the consequentialist view provides little insight into the moral significance of the values that research may endanger. The same utilitarian calculations that justify certain kinds of research that are invasive of individual privacy could be used to justify other less acceptable privacy invasions; highly objectionable police investigative activities, for example, could be justified in terms of the fundamental "social benefit" of national security.[17] To allow any invasions of privacy on risk-benefit grounds could have deleterious effects on social policy by contributing to a callous attitude toward invasions of citizen privacy generally. Even if research results entail significant social benefits, the countervailing negative consequences of the methods employed may outweigh those benefits and so render the study morally unjustifiable.

Moreover, a number of philosophers, among them Alasdair MacIntyre, take the position that "a project whose benefits clearly outweighed its risks might nevertheless be morally impermissible if the risks are unjustly borne by economically disadvantaged members of society."[18] The principle of distributive justice is invoked as a protection against "group risk," the risk that the interests of collectivities might suffer some future setback as a result of research study. In *Ethics in Social Research,* Robert Bower and Priscilla de Gasparis argue that,

> the standard use in quantitative social research (even that which is not focused on particular groups) of group characteristics—age, sex, race, marital status, income, and so on—as explanatory variables is apt to lead to the presentation of research results in ways that are ideally suited to the identification of intergroup differences and the drawing of comparisons that may seem invidious with respect to one group or favorable for another.[19]

Minority group members and people at lower socio-economic levels in society (the favorite subjects of social analysis, including socio-historical analysis) are particularly vulnerable to this kind of social injury.

Another difficulty posed by risk-benefit analysis is finding a common standard in terms of which to compare harmful and beneficial consequences. Risk-benefit analyses are useful guides to anticipated conduct only if they are performed in advance of the research project under consideration. The uncertainty of risks and benefits is implicit in Kuhn's description of the nature of scientific discovery, according to which the risks of social research are often not only incalculable, but often emerge accidentally in the course of the work and are identified after the fact as "unanticipated consequences."[20] Social researchers such as Joan Cassell argue that the advance assessment of risks and benefits requires predictions that cannot reliably be made in the unstable environment of social research.[21] One can speculate as to the benefits that may result from research, just as one can speculate as to some of the risks that record subjects may experience. But such risks and benefits currently resist quantitative analysis.

The judgments concerning the potential harm a research project presents to record subjects that can be made ahead of time tend to be based on untested assumptions about record subjects' feelings on the matter, or on the researcher's (or the review committee's) own sense of right and wrong. The notion of harm implies an evaluative framework for assessing damages to individuals and to social groups, one that

> entails fundamental assumptions about the nature of persons and society, about the individual and collective conditions constituting well-being, or its absence, about what is most and least valued by persons, groups, professions, and governments, and about the specific impact of social research on these constituencies."[22]

However much may be assumed about the harms and benefits record subjects would themselves see as important to them, very little is actually known about such matters, because most of the factors that must be considered are intangible and subjective. Tom Beauchamp asks, "should the term [harm] be restricted to physical consequences that are damaging and irreversible, or should it also embrace impermanent and less dramatic psychological effects? Legal effects? Economic effects?"[23]

The risk-benefit analysis is most effective in situations where the total benefit or cost expected from a particular course of action can be identified and measured with precision. Such precision is unrealistic in the evaluation of social research primarily because the harmful consequences that can be reasonably predicted are more likely to be cumulative in nature. In calculating the effects of breaking a promise of confidentiality, for example, we need to take into account not only the harm caused to the individual whose confidence has been violated, but the larger effect of the broken promise in undermining interpersonal trust in society. The accumulation of promise-breaking may damage an individual's self-esteem; but it may also lower the level of societal trust and undermine the integrity of the rule of promise-keeping which is essential to harmonious and effective social interaction.[24]

Since cumulative effects are not easily proven, researchers frequently fail to take them into account, limiting their calculations of harm to the individual subject(s). Although, as Donald Warwick notes with some irony, "they will often cite the cumulative beneficial effects of increased knowledge." The fact that researchers do not consider the negative effect of continual violations of individual rights to privacy is no indication that such harms do not exist. As Warwick darkly observes: "Those who take a different view of human nature, of the persistence of ruptured trust . . . will come to other conclusions."[25]

Given the problems with applying a strictly consequentialist analysis to the moral evaluation of social research, Herbert Kelman has proposed an alternative, rights-based analysis, one based on a description of a particular action, rather than on the prediction of its consequences.[26] The ultimate criterion for moral evaluation identified by Kelman is "consistency with human dignity," defined as "the status of individuals as ends in themselves, rather than as means towards some extraneous ends," a definition deriving from Kant's categorical imperative to "act so that in your own person as well as... every other you are treating mankind . . . as an end, never merely as a means."[27] According to this imperative, individuals ought never to be used to achieve goals that do not give primary consideration to their own goals. Kelman distinguishes two components—identity and community—which serve as conditions of dignity:

> identity refers to our capacity to take autonomous action, to distinguish ourselves from others, to live our lives on the basis of our own goals and values; community refers to our inclusion in an interconnected network of individuals who care for each other and protect each other's interests.[28]

Identity is here equated with individual freedom, community with individual justice. Kelman argues that to deny individuals identity or community is to treat individuals as means rather than as ends and so deprive them of their dignity.

This conception of human dignity places it within a consequentialist framework because it is linked to, and derived from, principles demanding the fulfillment of human potentialities; respect for dignity is important because it has consequences for an individual's capacity to express and develop himself or herself.[29] Nevertheless, although it is rooted ultimately in principles demanding fulfillment of human potentialities, respect for dignity can be treated as though it were an end in itself in moral decision making because the principle obtains even in the absence of demonstrable consequences for self-fulfillment. The crucial point in a rights-based analysis is that although the origin of such rights is ultimately rooted in harm-benefit considerations these rights become, "functionally autonomous ... [t]hat is, the right has moral force regardless of whether, in any given case, it can be *demonstrated* that its violation would cause harm."[30]

According to Kelman, we take or avoid certain actions defined by general moral principles not only to avoid causing harm, but to conform to, and maintain the integrity of, a right because of the presumed long-term systematic consequences of its violation. The principles of privacy and confidentiality derive their moral force from the presumption that the actions they proscribe have adverse consequences for the individual capacities and social conditions that are essential prerequisites to personal fulfillment; they are designed to protect record subjects and the society at large against the possibility of unforeseeable, as well as foreseeable, harm. Kelman argues persuasively that:

> If they [privacy and confidentiality] were made conditional on calculation of the magnitude of harm anticipated [by disclosure] they would lose much of their protective value. ... It is presumed that any violation [of the right to privacy] is damaging—if not in the short run, then in the long run; if not to the particular individual involved, then to the larger society (by weakening an important protective mechanism).[31]

For that reason, "it is enough to say that the right is being violated; there is no need to prove that its violation causes measurable harm."[32]

Within this modified harm-benefit framework, invasion of privacy generally and violation of confidentiality specifically may be viewed as harms of a special type as well as conditions that leave people vulnerable to the possibility of harm. Invasion of privacy cannot be described as a harm in the obvious sense of a lasting injury or measurable damage to the record subjects. It can, however, be subsumed under the category of harms that Alasdair MacIntyre designates "moral wrongs," acts that subject people to the experience of being morally wronged, whether or not their interests are damaged in specifiable ways.[33] Research that is invasive of individual privacy is wrong because it bypasses the normal decision-making capacities of individuals and interferes with the voluntary nature of their actions.

In terms of Kelman's analysis, invasion of privacy, by violating people's autonomy, is inconsistent with respect for their dignity and therefore a presumptive, or *prima facie* cause of harm. Privacy provides people with some protection against harmful or unpleasant experiences, against threats to the integrity and autonomy of the self, against embarrassment or lowered self-esteem. Invasions of privacy not only subject individuals to the possibility of harm; they increase the likelihood of harm because they deprive the individual of protection against it.[34]

An obvious source of concern about the potential invasiveness of socio-historical research specifically is the risk of public exposure in the event that information in individually identifiable records is disseminated beyond the research setting. Such exposure may subject individuals to the possibility of damaging consequences if such information becomes accessible to authorities who are in a position to penalize or harass them. Welfare recipients, whose private lives are always subject to scrutiny, or other captive populations (children, prisoners, the mentally infirm), are among those who are particularly vulnerable to such exposure. Even if the risk of penalty or reprisal is minimal or nonexistent, there remains the possibility that exposure will subject record subjects to embarrassment or disapproval and affect people's reputations.[35] Such negative social effects become a significant possibility when several sources of data are combined for new analysis. Public exposure also presents risks to particular collectivities who may be under study. Studies involving social or ethnic minority communities carried out by researchers with insufficient understanding of the cultural context, for instance, could have damaging consequences. Members of these groups may view the dissemination of information obtained in such studies as invasive of their group's privacy, with the result of reinforcing negative stereotypes about them.[36]

The distinguishing feature of much socio-historical research is that the data consist of information obtained from or about individuals on an earlier occasion and for a different purpose. When assessing the harms that may result from such research, the issue of consent is invariably raised. The notion of consent derives from the tort law on assault and battery which prohibits unlawful touching without an individual's authorization. "Informed consent" is a more recent concept, which was first explicated in the Nuremberg Code. Drafted in response to the international community's horror at Nazi medical experimentation, the Code outlines the conditions under which individuals may be presumed capable of exercising free power of choice without undue inducement or any element of fraud, force, duress, or other form of constraint or coercion. The major elements of informed consent include competence, voluntarism, full information, and comprehension.

The doctrine of informed consent is a reminder of the categorical imperative against violations of autonomy—the use of people as means rather than as ends in themselves. According to Alexander Capron,

> [t]heoretically, consent overcomes the means/ends problem because the subject who has truly consented has adopted the goals of the research program as his own; as a "collaborator" with the investigators, the subject is no longer a means to someone else's ends, but a participant in a process to reach his own ends. Alternatively, if the subject does not recognize the ends of the research

project to be merged with his own, at least it can be said that the subject has consented to being used as a means.[37]

Many of the ethical problems associated with social research can be obviated if the informed consent of record subjects can either be obtained or assumed by researchers, because consent satisfies the moral requirement of respect for persons.

With regard to research uses of administrative records, the question is whether we can assume tacit or implied consent on the part of the individual who originally supplied the information to subsequent uses of that information. The notion of implied consent is based on the assumption that the context in which information is originally collected can indicate a person's implicit or informal consent to subsequent disclosures. Individuals are, or should be, aware of the possibility that some of the personal information they provide to certain government agencies may be disclosed for use in auditing or in response to a court order or legislative inquiry, or for tax or other law enforcement purposes. Some would argue that individuals should also be aware of the fact that personal information may be used for subsequent statistical analyses by government agencies, since such analyses are routinely performed and are often reported in the press. This awareness, it is argued, therefore, may be taken as a kind of implied or tacit consent on the part of the individual who supplied the information to subsequent uses of it for a variety of purposes, including research and statistical purposes. The treatment of research and statistical uses of government-held personal information as a "routine use," as is done in some government jurisdictions, is a variation on this notion of implied consent.[38]

The assumptions surrounding the application of implied consent or "routine use" concepts to permit the disclosure of personal information for research or statistical purposes are seldom justified, as Arthur Miller makes clear:

> To talk of information being "voluntarily" given in the context of a police interrogation, an application for welfare payments, an employment relationship, or a psychological experiment is to ignore reality. . . . Even a questionnaire sent out under the imprimatur of a federal agency has an intimidating effect on some people, a weakness that often is played upon by the agency in its follow-up practices.[39]

Certain government services require that individuals provide what is often extremely personal information about themselves. Since they must disclose that information in order to receive benefits or compensation, for example, medical coverage, welfare, or unemployment insurance, there is some question whether such disclosure can be taken as "implied consent" to any use of that information; certainly it has not been given freely, which is what consent implies. Further, assuming individuals did not know that information they disclosed about themselves would be used in a different context, their capacity to protect their interests was clearly impaired when they consented to provide the information in the first instance.

The invasion of privacy that results from the failure to obtain consent for a clearly different use of the information than the one originally agreed to may be exacerbated by the breaking of a promise of confidentiality that was made, either explicitly or implicitly at the time the information was originally collected. The moral rule against breaking a promise of confidentiality is rooted in respect for individuals' autonomy over information about themselves, as well as respect for the integrity and importance of the confidential relationship in which such information is shared. The foundation of trust on which confidential relationships rely is critical both to the individual and to society as a whole because, without some control over who they will share personal information with, individuals would be unable to maintain privacy or protect themselves against harm; and by providing such a refuge, society benefits by maximizing individuals' capacity to fulfill their potential.

The obligation to protect confidentiality is binding on those who accept the information in confidence. Sissela Bok asserts that once a promise of confidentiality is made, "we no longer start from scratch in weighing the moral factors of a situation. They matter differently, once the promise is given, so that full impartiality is no longer called for."[40] In particular kinds of confidential relationships, for example, the relationship between therapist and patient or between social worker and client, the principle of confidentiality is defended on the grounds that it provides individuals with a safe area into which they can enter in order to seek help or obtain justice. Such a relationship imposes on the person who receives confidential information an affirmative duty with respect to the interests of the person who discloses it. The central affirmation of the relationship is that the vulnerability of the patient or client will not be exploited; the failure to protect their interests constitutes a form of abandonment.

The Kantian argument that people should be treated as ends in themselves and not merely as means requires that we show respect for the humanity and dignity of all persons and that we treat each other in accordance with those principles that express conduct we believe should be universally practiced. According to the moral philosopher Richard Hare, an acceptable moral judgment must satisfy the requirements of "prescriptivity" and "universalizability:"

> When we are trying, in a concrete case, to decide what we ought to do, what we are looking for ... is an action to which we can commit ourselves (prescriptivity) but which we are at the same time prepared to accept as exemplifying a principle of action to be prescribed for others in like circumstances (universalizability). If, when we consider some proposed action, we find that, when universalized, it yields prescriptions which we cannot accept, we reject this action as a solution to our moral problem—if we cannot universalize the prescription, it cannot become an "ought."[41]

The principle of confidentiality is a specific application of the principle of promise-keeping in ethics generally. To break a promise is to implicitly condone promise-breaking and, therefore, to contribute to the erosion of promise-keeping as a principle. In order to determine whether it is acceptable to break a promise, we need to ask ourselves what the world would be like if the principle of promise-breaking became part of everyone's nature. Would we choose to live in a world in which individuals were routinely permitted to break promises if doing so would produce knowledge they thought was worth having?

The respect due to persons and to existing relationships, and the importance of maintaining the integrity of promise-keeping as a principle, create strong *prima facie* reasons to support a duty of confidentiality. The moral premises justifying confidentiality do not, of course, foreclose debate over such questions as whether a promise of confidentiality should have been given in the first place, whether the promise is binding, and what circumstances justify overriding it. The legitimacy of confidentiality's moral premises can be overridden, for example, when the withholding of information could endanger the lives of the individuals themselves or innocent third persons. The crucial point is that in the absence of a competing moral imperative requiring disclosure, promises of confidentiality should be maintained.

The potentially invasive uses of personal information for socio-historical research also create ethical problems at the level of wider social values, by reducing the amount of private space possible for individuals within society. The preservation of individual moral autonomy is dependent on the maintenance of a physical and psychological boundary between the private and public domains. The practice of opening individually identifiable records to research, thereby widening the availability of personal information, may weaken the boundaries that society tries to sustain between these separate domains because it reinforces people's sense that personal information will, sooner or later, become publicly known. Moreover, research that reduces the level of privacy in society may cause diffuse harm independent of its effect on individual record subjects or the groups from which they are drawn. The atmosphere of surveillance created by the reduction of privacy generally may, in turn, contribute to the weakening of public trust on which the integrity of certain social institutions and social relations are based. Taken together with the proliferation of data banks and other records maintained on individuals, invasions of individual privacy in the interests of social research of various kinds may encourage a tendency to live "for the record."

A rights-based analysis requires that social research involving human subjects be judged within a framework of moral reasoning that focuses on principles that are shared between people and to which we can imagine people contractually agreeing. Such a framework returns us to the idea of the social contract that is implicit in the relationship between citizens and the state. In the interest of that social contract, individuals are obliged to surrender a certain amount of their privacy in return for the delivery of various social goods. The permission we give to the government to collect and store personal information is not unqualified; however, such a permission does not, for example, extend to allowing the government unlimited power over subsequent uses of such information. The collection of personal information by governments presents an agonizing moral dilemma concerning the appropriate balance between conflicting rights—individual rights versus the rights of the state to intrude into the lives of its citizens to promote and protect a range of societal interests. It qualifies as a moral dilemma, however, only because we accept, albeit in varying degrees, that the government possesses certain rights that may, in particular cases, legitimately override the rights of individuals.

Social researchers do not possess any comparable right of access to government-held personal information. No general contractual agreement exists between the research community and the public at large and in the absence of such a contract, social researchers have no moral right to their investigations corresponding to the rights of government. As Terry Pinkard makes clear, "at best [they] can argue that the studies will have some great yield (in social utility, for example) and should be supported. But [they] cannot validly argue that the investigation should be supported even in face of its violating individual rights to privacy by intruding into our 'safe' areas."[42]

Rights are our most demanding moral rules. In *Taking Rights Seriously,* Ronald Dworkin argues that:

> Individuals have rights when, for some reason, a collective goal is not a sufficient justification for denying them what they wish, as individuals, to have or to do, or not a sufficient justification for imposing some loss or injury upon them.[43]

If, as Dworkin maintains, rights "trump" utility, then they certainly trump the needs and interests of researchers, because "the citizen who bears a right does not hold a privilege and is not subject to the charity or professional etiquette of another."[44] If we cast this argument more specifically in terms of research access to government records containing personal information, it follows that privacy interests must take precedence over research interests in access when the two conflict.

In the same way that restrictions on the admissibility of evidence impede police work or limits on the use of confidential information hamper financial institutions, the application of stringent procedures for the administration of access to personal information in government archives will undoubtedly hinder and perhaps render impossible valuable research. Such a consequence is hardly welcome. But any ethical stance constrains someone's freedom; that does not mean such a stance is unreasonable or unjust. In the end, our acceptance of limitations on the pursuit of knowledge in order to protect a greater common interest is what distinguishes us as moral beings.

Margaret Cross Norton, one of the most articulate and comprehensive explorers of the ideas underlying the administration of government archives, has argued convincingly that the first principle in the care of public records is that, under a democratic form of government, the people are sovereign:

> ... that is, the records of the government belong to the people and the official who creates, files, and services the records is merely acting as custodian for the people ... officials do not own the records which they create, but merely act as custodians of the records on behalf of the people.[45]

Implicit in this custodial role is the archivists' trusteeship of the records in their custody. This aspect of the archivist's role is emphasized by S. N. Prasad, who states that the archivist's "ultimate allegiance ... is neither to the existing administration, nor to the scholars of today. His allegiance is to the records and to documentation, which he holds in sacred trust for the generations to come."[46] When the Society of American Archivists drafted its definition of an archivist in 1984, it also reaffirmed Sir Hilary Jenkinson's 1922 definition of the archivist as "a kind of Public Trustee,"[47] when it averred, "the archivist is the trustee of the present and the past for future generations ... a steadfast keeper of the records held in trust."[48]

In that capacity, archivists are charged with the responsibility to safeguard the integrity of the records in their custody—a responsibility that carries with it an implicit obligation to protect the integrity of particular relationships between citizens and their government to which the records bear witness and to intercede on behalf of record subjects in the administration of access to such records. Virginia Stewart underlines this point in her discussion of public welfare case files:

> the archivist has the immediate responsibility for maintaining rigorous standards in the protection of personal privacy on behalf of persons who may be unable to assert their rights—because they are legally incompetent to do so (children, institutionalized persons) or because they

are unaware that records involving them have been transferred to an archives.[49]

The SAA Code of Ethics for Archivists similarly directs archivists to "respect the privacy of individuals who created or are the subject of records and papers, especially those who had no voice in the disposition of materials."[50]

Privacy invasion is damaging both to the climate of a free society and to the integrity of the profession that permits it. Higher standards for administering access to archival records containing personal information need to be set out of concern for the integrity of research itself, as much as for the individuals whose lives it touches. Archivists have a particular obligation to alert the research community to the fact that, although some invasions of privacy are inevitable, a cavalier attitude toward such losses may, in Ruth Gavison's words, "corrupt the invader as well as harm the victim."[51]

In a paper presented to the Society of American Archivists' annual general meeting in 1982, Gerald Grob observed that:

> ... the tendency of most scholars has been to make their claim for access take precedence over all other rights, a position that is both irresponsible and dangerous. A system that rests solely on good intentions is, in effect, no system; there are few individuals who would admit to harboring anything but the best of intentions. Consequently it is imperative that [historians] recognize that the interests of different groups, each with different concerns, must be taken into account.[52]

Documenting the history of what are euphemistically called the "nonelites" of society increasingly requires that historians scrutinize the private lives of citizens who are powerless to object. And while the social historians' intentions may be of the purest kind—to expose inequities and so symbolically redress them—by the very nature of their endeavor they exploit further the powerlessness of those who become the subject of their inquiry, by abusing their right to privacy.

In its tacit approval of research and its goals, society endorses the role played by the research community and recognizes certain privileges. These privileges are, however, susceptible to abuse. Certain kinds of research may affect the interests, autonomy, and rights of record subjects in morally significant ways, which researchers, with their interest in producing knowledge, may undervalue or ignore. If record subjects' interests, specifically, their interest in privacy, are to be protected, archivists must promulgate stringent policies and procedures for the administration of records containing personal information, to ensure that violations of privacy are minimized and, wherever possible, eliminated. While recognizing the vital importance of research to human progress, the central affirmation of such policies must be that consideration for the welfare and integrity of individuals generally, and their right to privacy specifically, must prevail over the advancement of knowledge. Ruth Simmons believes, "[t]he time is over for ad hoc decisions on access, both for the protection of the repository and for the protection of privacy rights of individuals archivists are ethically and legally bound to uphold."[53] The question that remains now is, what specific steps do archivists need to take to ensure the protection of individual rights to privacy?

Notes

1. *Calgary Herald,* 13 February 1986: A22; *Globe and Mail* 11, February 1986: A21; *Winnipeg Free Press* 11, February 1986: 16.

2. Emile Durkheim, *The Elementary Forms of the Religious Life,* trans. Joseph Ward Swain (London: George Allen & Unwin, 1915), 429.

3. Herbert Kelman, "Ethical Issues in Different Social Science Methods," *Ethical Issues in Social Science Research,* eds. Tom L. Beauchamp et al. (Baltimore, Md.: Johns Hopkins University Press, 1982), 48.

4. Bok, *Secrets* (see chapt. 1, n.51), 235.
5. Paul Davidson Reynolds, *Ethical Dilemmas and Social Science Research* (San Francisco: Jossey-Bass, 1979), 230.
6. William Spinrad, "Academic Freedom," in *Civil Liberties* (Chicago: Quadrangle Press, 1970), 235.
7. Thomas S. Kuhn, *The Structure of Scientific Revolutions*, 2nd ed. (Chicago: University of Chicago Press, 1970), 68.
8. See Reynolds, *Ethical Dilemmas and Social Science Research*, 228-29.
9. Beauchamp, "Introduction," *Ethical Issues in Social Science Research*, eds. Beauchamp et al., 14.
10. John A. Robertson, "The Social Scientist's Right to Research and the IRB System," *Ethical Issues on Social Science Research*, eds. Beauchamp et al., 356.
11. Robert Craig Brown, "Government and Historian: A Perspective on Bill C-43," *Archivaria* 13 (Winter 1981-82): 123.
12. Bok, *Secrets*, 237-38.
13. See, for example, N. Peterson, "Forbidden Knowledge," *The Social Contexts of Research*, ed. S. Z. Nagi and R. G. Corwin (New York: John Wiley, 1972), 289-322.
14. Quoted in Robert T. Bower and Priscilla de Gasparis, *Ethics in Social Research: Protecting the Interests of Human Subjects* (New York: Praeger, 1978), 4.
15. Christian Bay, "Access to Political Knowledge as a Human Right," *Government Secrecy in Democracies*, ed. Itzhak Galnoor (New York: New York University Press, 1977), 23.
16. Kelman, "Ethical Issues in Different Social Science Methods," 88.
17. R. Jay Wallace, Jr., "Privacy and the Use of Data in Epidemiology," *Ethical Issues in Social Science Research*, eds. Beauchamp et al., 279.
18. Alasdair MacIntyre, "Risk, Harm, and Benefit Assessments as Instruments of Moral Evaluation," *Ethical Issues in Social Science Research*, eds. Beauchamp et al., 181.
19. Bower and de Gasparis, *Ethics in Social Research*, 29.
20. Ibid., 47.
21. Joan Cassell, "Does Risk-Benefit Analysis Apply to Moral Evaluation of Social Research?" *Ethical Issues in Social Science Research*, eds. Beauchamp et al., 144-62.
22. Donald P. Warwick, "Types of Harm in Social Research," *Ethical Issues in Social Science Research*, eds. Beauchamp et al., 103.
23. Tom Beauchamp, "Introduction," *Ethical Issues in Social Science Research*, eds. Beauchamp et al., 24.

24. Kelman, "Ethical Issues in Different Social Science Methods," 42.
25. Warwick, "Types of Harm in Social Research," 103.
26. Kelman, "Ethical Issues in Different Social Science Methods," 42.
27. Immanuel Kant, *The Fundamental Principles of the Metaphysics of Ethics,* trans. O. Manthey-Zorn (New York: Appleton-Century-Crofts, 1938), 47.
28. Kelman, "Ethical Issues in Different Social Science Methods," 43.
29. Ibid., 41, 43.
30. Ibid., 89.
31. Ibid.
32. Ibid., 46.
33. MacIntyre, "Risk, Harm, and Benefit Assessments," 177.
34. Kelman, "Ethical Issues in Different Social Science Methods," 48.
35. Ibid., 58.
36. Ibid.
37. Alexander Morgan Capron, "Is Consent Always Necessary in Social Science Research?" *Ethical Issues in Social Science Research,* eds. Beauchamp et al., 220.
38. The U. S. Department of Health, Education, and Welfare, for example, considers statistical analysis by qualified individuals as a "routine use" for some record systems. See Title 45 C.F.R. 5, Appendix B (101).
39. Miller, *Assault on Privacy* (see chapt. 1, n.13), 186.
40. Bok, *Secrets,* 120.
41. Richard M. Hare, "Moral Reasoning," excerpted in *Ethics: Theory and Practice,* ed. Manuel Velasquez and Cynthia Rostankowski (Englewood Cliffs, N.J.: Prentice-Hall, 1985), 98.
42. Terry Pinkard, "Invasions of Privacy in Social Science Research," *Ethical Issues in Social Science Research,* eds. Beauchamp et al., 270.
43. Ronald Dworkin, *Taking Rights Seriously* (Cambridge, Mass.: Harvard University Press, 1978), xi.
44. Pinkard, "Invasions of Privacy in Social Science Research," 267. John A. Robertson and E. L. Patullo argue that there may be constitutional grounds under the first amendment to perform research but as Terry Pinkard makes clear, there are no moral or legal grounds whatever that would support a right to perform research sufficient to override individual rights to privacy. See Robertson, "The Social Scientist's Right to Research and the IRB System," *Ethical Issues in Social Science Research,*

356-72; and E. L. Patullo, "Modesty is the Best Policy: the Federal Role in Social Research," *Ethical Issues in Social Science Research*, 373-90.

45. Margaret Cross Norton, *Norton on Archives*, ed. Thornton Mitchell (Carbondale, Ill.: Southern Illinois University Press, 1975), 26, 32.

46. S. N. Prasad, "The Liberalisation of Access and Use," in *Archivum: International Review on Archives*, 26, Proceedings of the 8th International Congress on Archives, Washington, 27 September—1 October 1976 (Munich: K. G. Saur, 1979), 143.

47. Sir Hilary Jenkinson, *A Manual of Archive Administration* (Oxford: Clarendon Press, 1922), 39.

48. "Archivist: A Definition," *S.A.A. Newsletter* (January 1984): 4.

49. Stewart, "Problems of Confidentiality" (see chapt. 4, n.42), 398.

50. *American Archivist* 43 (Summer 1980): 414.

51. Gavison, "Privacy and Limits of Law" (see chapt. 1, n.9), 470.

52. Gerald N. Grob, "Archivists and Historians: Problems of Appraisal," paper delivered at the Annual Meeting of the Society of American Archivists, Boston, 20 October 1982, quoted in Ruth Simmons, "The Public's Right to Know and the Individual's Right to be Private," *Provenance* 1 (Spring 1983): 2.

53. Ruth Simmons, "The Public's Right to Know and the Individual's Right to be Private," *Provenance* 1 (Spring 1983): 3.

Administering Access to Personal Information in Government Archives

Some Modest Proposals

> We must be exceptionally sensitive to our responsibilities to the public as users and to the public as subjects of our records. Modern records force the issue; and while it is possible—although expensive—to produce "public use versions" or "disclosure-free data sets," we still hold unparalleled information on our fellow citizens. We must make sure that our professional ethics are adequate to the challenge.
>
> Trudy Peterson, "Archival Principles and Records of the New Technology"

Archival professional ethics demand that, in administering access to records containing personal information, archivists demonstrate a sensitivity to the sensibilities of the individuals represented in the records and, more specifically, that they actively work toward ensuring the protection of the individuals' right to privacy. "Integral to the notion of proper archival management of records," Ruth Simmons argues, "... especially those which require decision making, is the necessity to demonstrate a pattern of practice which shows care and concern."[1] Proper archival management in the present context implies a number of obligations on the archivists' part. Among them are the obligations to strengthen and systematize policies and procedures for the administration of access to records containing personal information within their institutions; to learn about and debate privacy issues as a profession and to participate, through professional organizations, in improving the archival status quo in matters relating to privacy; and, lastly, to contribute, again as a profession, to the larger public debates concerning the protection of information privacy in an increasingly public society.

The archival management of access to personal information properly begins before records come into archival custody. At the time records are scheduled for transfer, the conditions under which they are to be held by the archives need to be clarified and documented. First, what details are available about the kinds of personal information contained in the records? Do statutory or other explicit provisions exist for protecting the confidentiality of such information? Are there any provisions requiring disclosure? If confidentiality provisions apply, are there any exceptions to the general rule of nondisclosure? What are these exceptions? What procedural and technical safeguards exist for protecting personal information? Who has the authority to decide whether access to records containing personal information is permissible for research or statistical purposes, and how are decisions to be documented, made known, and accounted for? At what point in time can the records safely be made generally available for research purposes? Archivists should be able to answer all these questions at the time records are scheduled for transfer to the archives and the answers should be routinely documented in records schedules and in any other transfer instruments.

In many cases, access restrictions will be determined by statute, regulation, or agency policy, in which case the basic decision as to the sensitivity of the records will already have been made. However, the defined restrictions may leave important questions unanswered (e.g., the duration of the restrictions, exceptions to the rule of nondisclosure). In these circumstances, the archivist responsible for transferring the records should clarify and, if necessary, expand on the restrictions in consultation with the record-creating agency to ensure that all relevant questions with respect to the nature and extent of restrictions are satisfactorily answered. Institutional guidelines for the protection of personal information in archival custody should also be developed to cover situations where either statute, regulation, or policy is silent on restrictions and where disclosure of the information would intrude on the privacy of individuals. The guidelines should identify the categories of information restricted for reasons of personal privacy, establish the duration of restrictions on general access, and specify the conditions under which access to records normally restricted to protect personal privacy will be allowed to accommodate research and statistical purposes.

In defining restrictions on access, archivists will need to keep in mind their professional obligation to justify any restrictions they place on access. Whatever decisions are taken with respect to restrictions, it is generally accepted that no distinction should be made between users, that is, archivists ought not to make judgments about the legitimacy of one type of research (or researcher) over another. They should be prepared to define and defend the moral principles on which limitations on access are based and publicize those limitations for the benefit of users through formal statements of access policy and in relevant finding aids. To ensure consistency in administering access to restricted records, standard operating procedures covering such areas as screening, withdrawal, cross-referencing, and periodic re-review of restricted records should be instituted.[2]

Determining the appropriate duration of restrictions on access requires a sensitivity on archivists' part—first, to the common law principle that rights to privacy do not diminish significantly over the lifetime of the individual to whom the information relates and second, to the common sense principle that, in some cases, these rights are not extinguished even with the death of that individual. For certain types of records that implicate substantial privacy values—social services case files are an obvious example—a closed period of 150 years from the birth of the individuals concerned is not an unreasonable restraint to place on general access. More detailed analyses of the nature of the privacy interests inherent in different types of records—court records, investigatory and law enforcement case files, school records, social services records of various kinds—as well as the types of harm implicated in their release are sorely needed if archivists are to develop guidelines for closed periods that are sufficiently sensitive to the varied privacy interests involved.

France's freedom of information law, which incorporates provisions allowing for graduated access to records implicating diverse privacy values, is a useful model on which a more refined system of closed periods might be built. Under the French law, documents containing medical information are closed for 150 years from the birth of the person concerned; personnel information is closed for 120 years from the person's birth; legal proceedings are closed for 100 years from the legal action or the closing of the dossier; individually identifiable statistical information is closed for 100 years; and other information which might threaten individual privacy is closed for 60 years from the date of the action involved. The French Council of State has fixed the list of documents to be included in the last category.[3]

Once the nature and extent of restrictions on access to records containing personal information have been established, there remains the matter of establishing a framework for reviewing requests for access to records restricted for reasons of personal privacy for research and statistical purposes.[4] Ethical review of research involving the use of such records is essential to minimize any adverse effects—both concrete and diffuse—that the research could have on individuals and on society as a whole. For most kinds of research involving human subjects, certain individual rights are generally accepted prerequisites for conducting the research. These include the right to be fully informed about the precise nature and purpose of the research in which participation is sought, so that consent may be given or withheld advisedly; the right to know about the risks and benefits involved in participation in the proposed research; and the right to assurance that privacy will not be invaded and that any information disclosed by the subject will remain confidential. In research that requires the use of records held in government archives, individuals are incapable of exercising these rights because they are unaware that records concerning them are being used for research purposes and because it is either impossible or impracticable to obtain their consent.

It is critical therefore that archivists intercede on behalf of record subjects to ensure that their rights to privacy are not violated. Unless the gain promised by research is very great relative to the loss of autonomy, it is unlikely that the community as a whole will accept ethical standards that give higher priority to research than to respect for record subjects. The ethical review process described in the following paragraph is adapted from the procedures for contracted access outlined in Chapter Five (particularly those of the U.S. National Archives and Records Administration and the National Archives of Canada) and includes many of the same features. However it also incorporates recommendations and guidelines for the conduct of research involving human subjects that have been developed by the U.S. Privacy Protection Study Commission, the Canada Council Consultative Group on Ethics, and the Medical Research Council of Canada.[5]

In the proposed review process, the primary responsibility for determining whether access to archival records restricted for reasons of personal privacy will be allowed for research or statistical purposes, and the conditions under which access will be granted, would be delegated to an ethical review board established under the authority of the head of the archival institution. The records that are subject to board-mediated review would be clearly established and defined in the board's mandate,[6] as would a mechanism for appealing board decisions. The board's obligations would be directed primarily at protecting the interests, autonomy, and rights of individuals represented in the records and secondarily at ensuring that harm to such individuals is avoided. To accomplish these ends, the board would screen research proposals, specify conditions on access, monitor the research process, and impose penalties for violations of access conditions.

To represent more equitably the interests at stake in the disclosure of records implicating privacy values, the board's membership would include at least one citizen advocate (e.g., a civil libertarian). If the records being requested concern an identifiable collectivity (e.g., a particular social, racial, or ethnic group), an advocate for that collectivity (e.g., a representative of a patients' rights group or a welfare rights organization) could act as the citizen advocate on the board. Other members would include a specialist in the relevant area of research who possesses a broad understanding of research design, a lawyer to provide legal expertise, the archivist responsible for the records requested, and an official of the record-creating agency. Although the membership of the review board will change, depending on the nature of the proposals brought forward to it, it is important that the board be a standing body that meets regularly to ensure the continuing review of research projects.

Ethical review of research involving the use of records that fall within the board's mandate will proceed as follows. Researchers wishing to have access to the records would submit the following:

- A written request to the board outlining the research proposal and design;
- A statement of the objectives of the research project,
- A detailed explanation of the methodology to be used;
- An explanation of why the research cannot be accomplished without personally identifiable information;
- A detailed statement of the administrative, technical, and physical safeguards to be used by the researcher

Personal Information in Government Archives 187

to prevent unauthorized use or disclosure of the information;
* A specification of how the information will be used, including a description of any proposed data linkages with other personally identifiable information and the source of data;
* An indication of the potential risks to record subjects if these are known; and
* A statement of any benefits to be derived from the research project.

In reviewing the research proposal, the review board will determine first whether disclosure of the records in personally identifiable form is necessary to accomplish the research or statistical purpose for which the disclosure is to be made, and second, whether the records requested contain information that was supplied or collected under an explicit or implicit expectation of confidentiality. Given the review board's focus on protecting the privacy rights of record subjects, records normally would be released for research or statistical purposes only when the use or disclosure did not violate a legitimate expectation of confidentiality on the part of the record subjects.

In determining whether or not an expectation of confidentiality on the part of record subjects is legitimate, the board will ask itself a number of questions. Were record subjects informed at the time the information was collected that the information they disclosed would be held confidential by the agency? Is there documentation supporting such a promise? Do any explicit statutory or other provisions exist that protect the confidentiality of the information? Do these provisions permit disclosure for research purposes? Can any precedents be cited for permitting, or denying, access for such purposes, and can these be considered determinative? Are the provisions specifically formulated for the protection of record subjects? Or are they designed more to protect generally defined agency interests during the active life of the records?

If no explicit confidentiality provisions exist, is there evidence to support an implicit expectation of confidentiality? For example, was the information disclosed in the context of a socially recognized confidential relationship? There are four basic criteria warranting the recognition of confidential communication: the communication must originate in confidence; the confidence is considered vital to maintaining the relationship; the relationship is one that should be encouraged; and the detriment to the relationship through fear of disclosure is greater than the benefit which would result from disclosure. A legitimate expectation of confidentiality may also be presumed when the information is of a particularly sensitive or intimate nature. As cases are reviewed and decisions appealed, formal guidelines for determining a legitimate expectation of confidentiality will begin to emerge.

The board will have the authority to determine whether, in a particular case, it is ethical for a presumption of confidentiality to be waived. The circumstances justifying the disclosure of confidential personal information for research purposes would have to be decided on a case by case basis, rather than defined *a priori*, to avoid discrimination against certain types of research; nevertheless, the circumstances should be narrowly circumscribed. For example, the argument that the research will advance knowledge should not, in itself, be considered determinative in favoring disclosure. To decide whether disclosure is justifiable, the review board will weigh the sensitivity of the information against the expectation of any tangible or compelling social benefit, primarily to the record subjects and secondarily to society as a whole. Although the potential benefits of research are a legitimate consideration, in balancing them against potential risks the board must give fuller consideration to the risks disclosure poses—both individual and collective—to physical, psychological, and humane values. Apart from weighing the potential benefits of research, the board will also take into account the currency of the records in determining whether an expectation of confidentiality can be waived. If the record subjects may reasonably be supposed deceased, the board may consider the threat to individual privacy to be sufficiently reduced to merit disclosure for research purposes.

The review board's fiduciary obligation to protect record subjects does not give it license to reject research proposals for any of the following reasons: 1) out of fear of embarrassment, either to the archives or to the record creating agency, from the publication of research results or out of fear of general political controversy; 2) based upon a political judgment that research results would, if published, harm a group, organization, or community and fear of the political consequences which might follow that harm; or, 3) based upon a judgment of the competence of a research investigator rather than of the particulars of a submitted research design. Such issues are more appropriately addressed in other social policy forums, for example, through the granting agency, through peer review, or through the political process at various levels.

Once the board determines either that disclosure will not violate a legitimate expectation of confidentiality or that it is ethical to waive confidentiality, it must then determine whether the research proposal is soundly designed in terms of its ability to achieve the stated research objectives, whether the methodology proposed by the researchers will permit them to obtain the projected research results without revealing personally identifying information; and, whether the technical and procedural safeguards proposed by the researcher will adequately protect the personal information.

The board's approval of a research proposal that meets all the criteria for disclosure will be conditional on the researchers' and all others associated with the research project who will have access to personally identifiable information from the records (as well as the manager of any data processing facility handling the records or data elements containing personal identifiers) agreeing to maintain the confidentiality of the information and to adhere to the conditions of access established by the board. These conditions will include:

- that personal information be rendered anonymous at the earliest possible time, ideally as soon as data are collected and verified;
- that records only be used for the purpose of the research project as described in the original proposal and not be used for any other purpose without the board's approval;
- that copies of records and any data elements which permit the identification of an individual or which can be identified with an individual not be transferred to any person or institution not directly involved with the research project;
- that no data linkages other than those specified in the original proposal and approved by the review board be made;
- that the administrative, technical, and physical safeguards against unauthorized use or disclosure outlined in the proposal be established by the researchers and followed by all persons associated with the project;
- that persons who are identified in the records not be contacted by, or on behalf of, the researcher without the authorization of the board;
- that copies of the records be destroyed or returned to the archives upon completion of the project (if the copies are destroyed, the researcher should verify this in writing to the board); and
- that any other conditions the board deems appropriate will also be adhered to.

Researchers who willfully violate any of the conditions on access imposed by the review board will be made subject to the same sanctions for disclosure as any government employee. Violations ought to be considered a breach of trust and prosecuted accordingly. Other penalties will include revoking the researcher's privileges at the archives and notifying the funding bodies, institutions, and professional associations or organizations with which the researchers and the research project are affiliated that the conditions of access have been breached. The researchers' acceptance of the conditions on access imposed by the review board, as well as their understanding of the penalties they risk incurring if any of the conditions are violated, will be attested to in a written agreement signed by both the board and the researchers.

As a defense against the compulsory disclosure of research records that are based on personal information obtained from an archives, the written agreement should also include a provision insulating the personal information from any uses other than research or statistical uses. The principle on which such a provision could be based is that of functional separation. First introduced by the U.S. Privacy Protection Study Commission in 1977, the principle of functional separation classifies records according to the function they perform—either the administrative function of providing the basis for individual decisions, determinations, or treatments affecting individuals, or the statistical-research function of providing a study base for defining groups and producing summary information about them.

Applying the principle as a formal rule underlying the disclosure of personal information would involve characterizing records used for research or statistical purposes as research-statistical records even when the information originates from administrative records. Once records were characterized as research-statistical records, they would not be allowed to be used for nonstatistical (i.e., administrative) purposes in identifiable form, subject to a few exceptions.[8] The Privacy Commission's report includes examples of statutory mechanisms for enforcing the principle of functional separation. Although directed primarily at records collected or maintained for research or statistical purposes, these mechanisms are amenable to adaptation for personally identifiable records that are used for research or statistical purposes.[9]

While researchers will be accountable to the review board for any changes in research design undertaken after board approval, the provider of the information, that is, the archives (and specifically the board), will have the primary obligation to ensure that researchers are complying with the conditions on access, particularly in those projects that may present more than minimal risk. At the time the proposal is approved, provision for continuing review will be made and the method of review determined in accordance with the risk the project poses to record subjects' interests; the justifications for the method chosen should be documented. At a minimum, the board will require that researchers provide progress reports to the board at regular intervals, updating the status of any approved project and indicating any design changes that might have occurred in the course of the research. Before the project is approved, researchers will also be required to provide a time line for the project, indicating approximately at what point the identifiers will be expunged so the board can check for compliance. For projects that present more than minimal risk, the board will arrange for the project to be audited by one of its members, or a delegate, at a designated interval(s).

The practical benefits of a coherent policy and clearly defined procedures for administering access to records containing personal information that establish the nature and extent of access restrictions, define standard operating procedures for managing the records, and specify the conditions under which access to restricted records for research or statistical purposes is permissible, cannot be underestimated. They ensure the consistent protection of record subjects' privacy rights, and they also advance other archival program objectives, among them the creation of an equitable environment for access, the identification and classification of confidential records that come into archival custody, and the maintenance of cooperative and consultative relationships with record-creating agencies. These additional benefits are underlined by Roland Baumann in his assessment of state archival policies for administering access to confidential records:

> The existence of a specific policy and established procedures for handling confidential records minimizes administrative uncertainty, enhances archival authority and responsibility in this domain, and speeds up the reference process to the benefit of all users. . . . A state

archives displaying appropriate initiative by offering agencies formal access procedures based on a reasonable approach . . . can reduce the variations in agency-imposed restrictions, enhance the understanding of research uses, and reduce the "undue amount of discretion agencies have in determining who will and who will not be allowed to examine public records."10

As Baumann further notes, a specific policy and established procedures reduce, too, the undue amount of discretion archivists themselves are sometimes inclined to exercise in their dealings with researchers seeking access to restricted records.11

Systematizing procedures may also result in more systematic transfers of hitherto inaccessible records to archival custody. In jurisdictions where the archives' right of access to government records for appraisal purposes is not mandated in legislation (and even in jurisdictions where it is), archivists are often refused access to records containing sensitive personal information which are either maintained by the record-creating agency in perpetuity or destroyed before archivists have had an opportunity to determine whether they have archival value.12

While the destruction of such records will guarantee that the privacy rights of record subjects are permanently protected, it might equally hinder the accomplishment of other fundamental rights. Danielle Laberge underlines this point in arguing against the specific destruction of Canadian juvenile criminal records:13

> if the immediate benefit produced by the systematic and complete destruction of juvenile criminal records is the protection of the privacy of the juveniles involved, in the long run, such action might well constitute a severe handicap to the realization of other rights. . . . including the right to adequate treatment when it is required, the right to be protected from undue judicial intervention, and the right to see collective wrongs re-dressed . . .14

The existence of a formal policy and related procedures that reflect an understanding of, and a sensitivity to, privacy interests might be an incentive for otherwise reluctant government agencies to allow archivists access to confidential records in order to appraise them, and, if they have archival value, arrange for their eventual transfer to the archives.

As the volume of electronic records coming into archives increases, archivists will also need to learn and apply a variety of technical procedures for anonymizing personally identifiable data; techniques such as deletion of identifiers, code linkage, brokerage systems, microaggregation, and random error inoculation.[15] The sophisticated nature of anonymization techniques suggests that archivists' level of competence in this area will need to be raised and that they will need to develop alliances with computer programmers to ensure that disclosure-free data sets are, in fact, disclosure free. Although procedures designed to protect confidentiality undoubtedly will result in some reduction in the quantity and quality of the data available for general use, they will not destroy the net value of the data. And, while research requests for access to personally identifiable records are unlikely to diminish in the near future, the research community is not insensitive to the fact that "The price paid now in caution, procedural development, and perhaps data imprecision is low compared to the costs to research targets that might flow from breaches of confidentiality."[16] As anonymization procedures are refined and improved, the research community's need for personally identifiable data may eventually decrease.

For most archivists, the dilemmas that arise from legitimate but conflicting interests—the individual's right to privacy and society's need for knowledge—present themselves in the workplace and require solutions within that institutional context through formalized policies and procedures such as those described in the previous paragraphs. This reality notwithstanding, it is also apparent that privacy concerns intersect with a wide range of ethical, legal, and administrative issues, all of which directly (and indirectly) affect archivists as communicators of society's documentary memory and as trustees of the records in their custody. It is unlikely that answers to the many questions these issues raise will be found by archivists working in isolation from one another. Their solutions require, rather, the collective participation and judgment of the archival profession. Archivists need to learn about and debate, as a profession, the ethical, legal, and administrative dimensions of privacy as an information management issue.

The organizational and educational structures necessary for addressing professional concerns related to privacy already exist in the form of national and regional archival organizations and through professional schools that teach archival science. The principles and concepts associated with administering access to personal information in archival custody, as well as the administrative and technical procedures for protecting personal information, could be included in the curriculum of professional archival education programs and addressed through special training workshops, seminars, or other types of programs sponsored by professional organizations. To enable archivists to respond in a thoughtful and informed manner to the various situations they confront in the course of administering access to records that implicate privacy values, ongoing privacy issues related to access, as well as threshold concerns, such as privacy act expungements and the ethical destruction or permanent closure of confidential records, should be debated regularly during the annual meetings of archival organizations as well as in professional journals. Standing ethics or professional standards committees within professional organizations could also be established, if these do not already exist, to sensitize and guide archivists making decisions about privacy issues, on the range of perceptions they should bring to bear, and the processes of decision making that should be observed. Such committees could also recommend ways and means of strengthening the profession's role in managing personal information.

Some of these ways and means are documented in the report of the Society of American Archivists Task Force on Goals and Priorities. In *Planning for the Archival Profession,* the SAA Task Force outlines a set of objectives for the profession designed to ensure, among other things, the availability and use of records of enduring value. One of the objectives calls for archivists to "initiate and/or support legislation, regulations and professional practices which allow maximum access to public and private records, while protecting individual and organizational rights and interests."[17] The steps necessary to achieve this objective are set out in a three-point strategy. Although its focus is primarily on increasing access to records of enduring value, the strategy can easily be adapted to promote privacy objectives.

According to the Task Force, before archivists can actively participate in initiating and supporting legislation that ensures an appropriate balance between access and privacy rights, they must first "evaluate the effect of laws, regulations, and archival procedures relating to access, duplication, and publication on the use of archival records."[18] As Alice Robbin's survey of the public policy issues associated with access to restricted records compellingly demonstrates, archivists need to become better informed about the statutory environment in which they work, if they hope to exercise any influence over that environment. The first point in the Task Force's strategy therefore requires that archivists investigate the impact of legislation on the use of records in public and private institutions; identify the laws, regulations, and court decisions which increase or decrease access and document institutional responses to legislation and litigation; study existing access practices and identify those records that present the greatest access and use problems; and identify institutional procedures for administering access to restricted records. [19]

Once archivists have a clearer picture of the statutory, regulatory, and administrative context in which records containing personal information are maintained, they could then work toward "secur[ing] the passage of laws and regulations . . . that ensure availability of records consistent with the protection of individual and organizational rights and interests."[20] The second step in the Task Force's strategy involves archivists building coalitions with affected groups—professional organizations, public officials, government agencies, users, and civil libertarians, as well as with lawyers and politicians—and working with these groups to draft model legislation. To accommodate privacy interests, a model access and/or privacy law should define, as a minimum requirement, the categories of personal information that are, and are not, exempt from access; establish a deadline for all restrictions; provide a balancing formula with specific criteria for weighing access and privacy rights concerning the disclosure of personal information; provide for research access under articulated safeguards; and establish the principle of functional separation as a formal rule underlying the disclosure of personal information for research or statistical purposes.[21]

Apart from securing legislation, archivists should formally articulate the basic ethical principles that should underlie the administration of access to personal information in archival custody. Alice Robbin has proposed a set of ethical standards for the protection of personal information held in data archives. The standards are equally appropriate to other kinds of archives, enshrining as they do archivists' commitment to principles that include a responsibility to protect the public trust with which personal information has been given; the maintenance of a high standard of professional competence with respect to the nondisclosure of confidential information; sensitivity to the social codes and moral expectations of the public community which they serve; safeguarding the confidentiality of personally identifiable information; establishing and publicizing conditions for protecting confidential records; and establishing appropriate security measures to prevent access to data processing and storage devices that maintain personal information.[22] Ethical standards serve a number of useful purposes: they are a valuable educational and training device for promoting discussion of privacy issues affecting archivists; in the event of violations of privacy in an archival context, they provide criteria or points of reference by which to assess situations; and they serve as a solid foundation on which to build more specific policies and procedures for the protection of personal information in archival custody.

Continuing review of laws and regulations affecting the archival administration of access to personal information is essential to minimize conflicts which may arise from a lack of clarity about rules, rights, and responsibilities. The third and final point in the Task Force's three-point strategy calls for professional organizations to establish mechanisms for the ongoing monitoring of laws and professional practices in the area of access, "in order to draft new legislation, modify existing legislation, develop models and guidelines, and otherwise take timely action."[23] Among other things, standing committees within professional organizations could monitor litigation, legal opinions, and statutory revisions in order to clarify access and privacy laws; draft model statements on access policy; develop general guidelines for closed periods; and establish continuing education programs that address privacy issues in a systematic way.

According to the traditional taxonomic model of professionalism, one of the attributes that characterizes a profession is "institutionalized altruism," which Richard Cox describes as "a structural system that promotes behavior of its practitioners beneficial to others. This type of service orientation includes concerns for staying abreast of developments in a field so that clients are not harmed and standards are maintained to protect clients."[24] One way in which the institutionalized altruism of the archival profession is made manifest is in its commitment to increasing access to records of enduring value while ensuring, at the same time, that various rights, including rights to privacy, are protected; the report of the SAA Task Force on Goals and Priorities reflects such a commitment. This altruism could also be expressed through a professional contribution to the larger public debates concerning the protection of personal privacy in an increasingly public society.

Archivists, along with records managers, should be at the forefront of those debates, questioning the technological and bureaucratic imperatives that require the collection and maintenance of so much personal information and challenging the assumption that, because the technological capacity to collect, store, and disseminate enormous amounts of personal information exists, it therefore ought to be exploited. As Richard Lytle warned back in 1972, "this doctrine of conventional wisdom is invalid in a society where 'needs' are often created and technological change has acquired such momentum that new technologies are adopted for their own sake."[25] Given the dangerous opportunities that modern technique affords, he argued, "[t]he archival profession should make a collective contribution toward a humane standard for data collection and dissemination."[26] Though they are intimately acquainted with the ethical dilemmas associated with collecting and maintaining enormous quantities of personal information, archivists have yet to make a substantial contribution to this area of public policy debate. The experience of archivists and records managers should be communicated to legislative bodies and other policymakers to ensure that the concerns of the professions are heard and to provide relevant audiences with information that will assist them in formulating and amending policies and making decisions on privacy matters affecting the recordkeeping environment.

In the same spirit of altruism, the archival profession should work toward ensuring a humane standard for the preservation of society's documentary memory. The argument that, because new technologies make it possible for archivists to preserve considerably more information than was previously possible, they therefore ought to preserve more, is simply another facet of the fallacious and dangerous conventional wisdom supporting and reinforcing technological imperatives. Storing vast quantities of information in a compact format is no solution to the problem of an overabundance of information; it merely perpetuates the problem and, in the process, increases exponentially threats to individual privacy. Rational and independent appraisal judgments, guided by clearly defined archival principles and concepts, have never been more urgently required. When making appraisal decisions, archivists need especially to bear in mind Hans Booms' cautionary observation that enduring values cannot be determined by the degree to which they satisfy the needs of present-day research, nor ascertained through "a futurology of research interests."[27] This observation becomes acutely pertinent when these present needs and future interests dictate value judgments that seem to measure the significance of documentary material as much by its quantifiability as by the societal processes the material reflects.

Like debates over certification or standardized archival practices, discussions about the ways and means through which archivists might clarify and enhance their role in administering access to personal information "relate to what it means to be a profession and have sufficient power to accomplish such goals."[28] According to Richard Cox, the seemingly insurmountable obstacles—poor resources, a general lack of authority, public recognition, or influence—frequently cited to explain the dearth of archival solutions to the complex problems created (or at least, exacerbated) by modern recordkeeping environments, demonstrate precisely why archivists need to explore the issue of professionalism in more depth. As Cox points out, "the archival community lacks resources and authority partly because it fails to assert itself as a profession fulfilling an essential role in modern society."[29] If archivists are to have any success in their efforts to resolve the myriad privacy dilemmas that present themselves in an archival context, it is clear they will need to equip themselves with the conceptual and ethical tools that will enable them to build community support and, ultimately, community sanction for the archival profession. The resources needed to develop and institute morally and legally defensible policies and procedures for managing personal information in archival custody, and the authority required to enforce them, are not likely to be forthcoming until archivists have cultivated, in a more systematic way, the habits of mind and shared values that characterize a profession.

Meanwhile, archivists can best assure an appropriate balance between the individual's right to privacy on the one hand, and society's need for knowledge on the other, by conducting themselves professionally in accordance with principles that satisfy the moral requirement of respect for persons. Respect for the humanity and dignity of all persons, and the self-containing sense of responsibility arising from it, are the forces that will guide archivists through the ethical dilemmas that present themselves when the competing values of individual autonomy and freedom of inquiry confront each other. The profession's success in reconciling this antinomy of late twentieth century liberal culture will depend on the breadth and depth of its commitment to those forces.

Notes

1. Ruth Simmons, "The Public's Right to Know and the Individual's Right to be Private," *Provenance* 1 (Spring 1983): 3.
2. For a detailed analysis of each of these areas, see Gary M. Peterson and Trudy Huskamp Peterson, *Archives and Manuscripts: Law* (Chicago: Society of American Archivists, 1985), 60-71.
3. Gloria D. Westfall, "Access to Official Information in Britain and France: A Study in Contrasts," *Collection Management* 6:1/2 (1984): 173. See also Michel Duchein, "Access to Archives in France," *Archives: The Journal of the British Records Association* 15:65 (April 1981): 26-29.
4. The U. S. Privacy Protection Study Commission defines research and statistical purposes as, "the developing and reporting of aggregate or anonymous information not intended to be used, in whole or in part, for making a decision about an individual that is not an integral part of the particular research project." See Privacy Protection Study Commission, *Personal Privacy in an Information Society* (see chapt. 2, n.38), 572.

5. See Privacy Protection Study Commission, *Personal Privacy in an Information Society* 567-604; Canada Council, Consultative Group on Ethics, *Ethics* (Ottawa: Canada Council, 1977); Medical Research Council of Canada, *Guidelines on Research Involving Human Subjects* (Ottawa: Minister of Supply and Services, 1987).

6. These will, necessarily, vary in accordance with the statutory or regulatory environment in which the archives operates. The U. S. NARA, for example, subjects to board-mediated review records containing personal information, the disclosure of which would constitute a clearly unwarranted invasion of privacy (e.g., information about the physical or mental health or medical or psychiatric care or treatment of the individual, and that relate to events less than 75 years old); whereas the National Archives of Canada reviews records containing personal information that are systematically organized or retrieved by the name of an individual or by an identifying number or symbol assigned to an individual (e.g., personal case files).

7. Retention, for example, for longitudinal studies, may be necessary, but it should be the exception and not the rule. Moreover, the decision to retain identifiers is not open to the discretion of researchers; it should be a matter for the review board to decide. If identifiers are retained, specific precautions—such as recording personal identifiers in a separate file that is cross-referenced to the rest of the data—should be required if these are not already included in the proposal.

8. The Commission argues, for example, that research records should not be immune from compulsory disclosure when a researcher or research institution is under investigation for possible violation of law and confidential records constitute the only valuable source of information necessary for the investigation. The Commission also argues that a statutory exception to the nondisclosure rule is necessary for auditing or evaluating government funded research and statistical activities.

9. See *Personal Privacy in a Information Society,* 579-81.

10. Baumann, "Administration of Access to Confidential Records," (see chapt. 4, n.44), 366-67. Baumann's article includes a useful checklist of questions that archivists should consider when determining an access policy for confidential records. See Baumann, 369.

11. Ibid., 367.

12. Archivists at one state archives surveyed by Roland Baumann were denied access for appraisal purposes to poten-

tially valuable records from three agencies: "each agency 'based its denial on the confidentiality of the records, which of course the agency plans to destroy'." See Baumann, "Administration of Access to Confidential Records," 364. See also Alice Robbin, "State Archives and Issues of Personal Privacy" (see chapt. 4, n.44), 173; and Ruth Simmons, "The Public's Right to Know and the Individual's Right to be Private," 2.

13. Ms. Laberge's arguments were directed against a provision in the 1983 Canadian Young Offenders Act authorizing the destruction of records created and maintained pursuant to the Young Offenders Act and its predecessor, the Juvenile Delinquents Act. Complying with the provision would have required that records already in archival custody be destroyed. The Act has since been amended and the provision requiring the destruction of all records repealed. See Young Offenders Act S.C. 1980-81-82-83, c.110, s.45; 1986, c.32, s.35.

14. Danielle Laberge, "Information, Knowledge and Rights: The Preservation of Archives as a Political and Social Issue," *Archivaria* 25 (Winter 1987-88): 44, 49.

15. Some of these techniques are discussed in Chapter Five. See pages 134-38, *supra*.

16. Richard I. Hoffebert, "Confidentiality, Privacy and Social Data Archives: Special Problems for Policy Analysis," *Archivists and Machine-Readable Records* (see chapt. 2, n.2), 228.

17. Society of American Archivists, *Planning for the Archival Profession: A Report of the SAA Task Force on Goals and Priorities* (Chicago: Society of American Archivists, 1986), Goal III, Objective C.

18. Ibid., Goal III, Objective C.1.

19. Ibid.

20. Ibid., Goal III, Objective C.2.

21. The Ontario Freedom of Information and Protection of Privacy Act (1987) provides a useful structure on which to develop a model law. See Chapter Three, pp. 85-88, *supra*. The amended Georgia Records Act has also been recommended as a model state law. For a description of the Georgia Act, see Baumann, "Administration of Access to Confidential Records," 364-66.

22. Alice Robbin, "Ethical Standards and Data Archives," in *Secondary Data: New Directions for Program Evaluation,* ed. Robert F. Boruch (San Francisco: Jossey-Bass, 1978), 15-17.

23. Society of American Archivists, *Planning for the Archival Profession,* Goal III, Objective C.3.

24. Richard Cox, "Professionalism and Archivists in the United States," *American Archivist* 49 (Summer 1986): 233.

25. Richard Lytle, Review of *The Assault on Privacy: Computers, Data Banks and Dossiers,* by Arthur Miller, *American Archivist* 35 (July-October 1972): 404.

26. Ibid., 405.

27. Hans Booms, "Society and the Formation of a Documentary Heritage: Issues in the Appraisal of Archival Sources," trans. and ed. Hermina Joldersma and Richard Klumpenhouwer, *Archivaria* 24 (Summer 1987): 92, 100.

28. Cox, "Professionalism and Archivists," 241.

29. Ibid.

Selected Bibliography

Adler, Allan, ed. *Litigation under the Federal Freedom of Information Act and the Privacy Act,* 14th ed. Washington, D.C.: American Civil Liberties Union Foundation, 1989.

Anderson, Joseph R. "Public Welfare Case Records: A Study of Archival Practices." *American Archivist* 43 (Spring 1983): 169-79.

Archivaria 14 (Summer 1980),"Archives and Social History," : 1-201.

"Archivist: A Definition." *SAA Newsletter* (January 1984): 4-5.

Arendt, Hannah. *The Human Condition.* Chicago: University of Chicago Press, 1958.

"Assessing FOIA." *Newsletter on Intellectual Freedom* 35 (January 1986): 6.

[Australia] Law Reform Commission. *Report No. 22: Privacy.* 3 vols. Canberra: Australia Government Publishing Service, 1983.

Bathory, Peter Dennis, and Wilson Carey McWilliams. "Political Theory and the People's Right to Know." In *Government Secrecy in Democracies,* edited by Itzhak Galnoor. New York: New York University Press, 1977.

Baumann, Roland M. "The Administration of Access to Confidential Records in State Archives: Common Practices and the Need for a Common Law." *American Archivist* 49 (Fall 1986): 349-70.

Bay, Christian. "Access to Political Knowledge as a Human Right." In *Government Secrecy in Democracies,* edited by Itzhak Galnoor. New York: New York University Press, 1977.

Beauchamp, Tom L. et al., eds. *Ethical Issues in Social Science Research.* Baltimore, Md.: Johns Hopkins University Press, 1982.

Bier, William C., ed. *Privacy: A Vanishing Value?* New York: Fordham University Press, 1980.

Bloustein, Edward J. "Privacy as an Aspect of Human Dignity: An Answer to Dean Prosser." *New York University Law Review* 39 (1964): 962-1007.

Bogue, Allan G. "Data Dilemmas: Quantitative Data and the Social Science History Association." *Social Science History* 3 (Oct. 1978): 204-26.

Bok, Sissela. *Secrets: On the Ethics of Concealment and Revelation.* New York: Vintage Books, 1983.

Boruch, Robert F., and Joe S. Cecil. *Assuring the Confidentiality of Social Research Data.* Philadelphia: University of Pennsylvania Press, 1979.

———. eds. *Solutions to Ethical and Legal Problems in Social Research.* New York: Academic Press, 1983.

Bower, Robert T., and Priscilla de Gasparis. *Ethics in Social Research: Protecting the Interests of Human Subjects.* New York: Praeger Publishers, 1978.

Breisach, Ernst. *Historiography, Ancient, Medieval and Modern.* Chicago: University of Chicago Press, 1983.

Brown, Michael, Brenda Billingsley, and Rebecca Shamai. *Privacy and Personal Data Protection: A Report on Personal Record Keeping by the Ministries and Agencies of the Ontario Government.* Toronto: Commission on Freedom of Information and Individual Privacy, 1980.

Brown, Robert Craig. "Government and Historian: A Perspective on Bill C-43." *Archivaria* 13 (Winter 1981-82): 119-23.

Burnham, David. *The Rise of the Computer State.* New York: Random House, 1983.

Canada. Department of Communications and the Department of Justice. *Privacy and Computers.* Report of a Joint Task Force. Ottawa: Information Canada, 1972.

———. Department of Justice. *Access and Privacy: The Steps Ahead.* Ottawa: Minister of Supply and Services, 1987.

——— Human Rights Commission. Privacy Commissioner. *Report of the Privacy Commissioner on the Use of the Social Insurance Numbers in Canada.* Ottawa: Department of Justice, 1981.

———. Information Commissioner. *Annual Report, 1984- .* Ottawa: Minister of Supply and Services.

——— Information Commissioner. "Main Brief to the House of

Commons Standing Committee on Justice and Legal Affairs from the Office of the Information Commissioner." May 7, 1986.
____. Parliament. *Access to Information Act and the Privacy Act.* S.C. 1980-81-82-83, c. 111, Sections I and II.
____. Privacy Commissioner. *Annual Report, 1984-* . Ottawa: Minister of Supply and Services.
____. Privacy Commissioner. *Aids and the Privacy Act.* Ottawa: Minister of Supply and Services, 1989.
____. Standing Committee on Justice and Solicitor General on the Review of the Access to Information Act and the Privacy Act. *Open and Shut: Enhancing the Right to Know and the Right to Privacy.* The Report of the Standing Committee on Justice and Solicitor General on the Review of the Access to Information Act and the Privacy Act. Ottawa: Queen's Printer, 1987.
____. Treasury Board. "Report on Data Matching." Presented in Hearings before the Standing Committee on Justice and Solicitor General on the Review of the Access to Information Act and the Privacy Act. May 3, 1985.
____. Treasury Board Secretariat. *Interim Policy Guide: Access to Information Act and the Privacy Act.* Ottawa: Minister of Supply and Services, 1983.
Canada Council. Consultative Group on Ethics. *Ethics.* Ottawa: Canada Council, 1977.
Canadian Association of University Teachers. "Freedom of Information: A Brief Submitted to the Government of Canada by the Canadian Association of University Teachers." 1978.
Carlson, Walter M. "Privacy." *Annual Review of Information Science and Technology* 12 (1977): 279-305.
Clark, Lorenne M. "Privacy, Property, Freedom and the Family." In *Philosophical Law: Authority, Equality, Adjudication, Privacy,* ed. Richard Bronaugh. Westport, Conn.: Greenwood Press, 1978.
"Code of Ethics for Archivists." *American Archivist* 43 (Summer 1980): 414-18.
Coker, Kathey Roe. "Confidentiality of Records and Access: A Survey of State Archival Institutions." *Records Management Quarterly* 16 (July 1982): 22-31.

Committee on the Records of Government. *Report of the Committee on the Records of Government.* Washington, D.C.: American Council of Learned Societies, Social Sciences Research Council, Council on Library Resources, March 1985.

Cooke, Anne. "A Code of Ethics for Archivists: Some Points for Discussion." *Archives and Manuscripts* 15 (November 1987): 95-104.

Council of Europe. *Convention for the Protection of Individuals With Regard to Automatic Processing of Personal Data.* Strasbourg: Council of Europe, 1981.

_____. *Explanatory Report on the Convention for the Protection of Individuals with Regard to Automatic Processing of Personal Data.* Strasbourg: Council of Europe, 1981.

Davis, Frederick. "What do we mean by 'right to privacy?'" *South Dakota Law Review* 4 (1959): 1-24.

"Draft bibliography on confidentiality." *SAA Newsletter* (May 1982): 10-11.

Duchein, Michel. *Obstacles to the Access, Use and Transfer of Information from Archives: A RAMP Study with Guidelines.* Paris: Unesco, 1983.

Dworkin, Ronald. *A Matter of Principle.* Cambridge, Mass.: Harvard University Press, 1985.

_____. *Taking Rights Seriously.* Cambridge, Mass.: Harvard University Press, 1978.

Flaherty, David H. "Access to Historical Census Data in Canada: A Comparative Analysis." *Canadian Public Administration* 20 (Fall 1977): 481-98.

_____. "The Bellagio Conference on Privacy, Confidentiality and the Use of Governmental Microdata." In *Secondary Analysis: New Directions for Program Evaluation,* ed. Robert F. Boruch. San Francisco: Jossey-Bass, 1978.

_____. "Privacy and Confidentiality: The Responsibility of Historians." *Reviews in American History* 8 (Sept. 1980): 419-29.

_____. *Privacy and Government Data Banks: An International Perspective.* London: Mansell Publishing, 1979.

_____. *Privacy in Colonial New England.* Charlottesville, Va.: University of Virginia Press, 1972.

———. *Research and Statistical Uses of Ontario Government Personal Data.* Toronto: Commission on Freedom of Information and Individual Privacy, 1979.

———, ed. *Privacy and Data Protection: An International Bibliography.* White Plains, N.Y.: Knowledge Industry Publications, 1984.

Fried, Charles. *An Anatomy of Values: Problems of Personal and Social Choice.* Cambridge, Mass.: Harvard University Press, 1970.

Gavison, Ruth. "Privacy and the Limits of the Law." *Yale Law Journal* 89(3) (Jan. 1980): 421-71.

Geda, Carolyn L., Erik W. Austin, and Francis X. Blouin, Jr., eds. *Archivists and Machine-Readable Records: Proceedings of the Conference on Archival Management of Machine-Readable Records,* February 7-10, 1979, Ann Arbor, Mich. Chicago: Society of American Archivists, 1980.

Geselbracht, Raymond H. "The Origins of Restrictions on Access to Personal Papers at the Library of Congress and the National Archives." *American Archivist* 49 (Spring 1986):142-62.

Gibson, Dale, ed. *Aspects of Privacy Law: Essays in Honour of John M. Sharp.* Toronto: Butterworths, 1980.

Gillis, Peter. "The Case File: Problems of Acquisition and Access from the Federal Perspective." *Archivaria* 6 (Summer 1978): 32-39.

Gough, J. W. *The Social Contract.* 2nd ed. Oxford: Clarendon Press, 1957.

Great Britain. Home Office. *Report of the Committee on Data Protection.* London: Her Majesty's Stationery Office, 1978.

———. *Report of the Committee on Privacy.* London: Her Majesty's Stationery Office, 1972.

Hamby, Alonzo L., and Edward Weldon, eds. *Access to the Papers of Recent Public Figures: The New Harmony Conference.* Bloomington, Ind.: American Historical Association, Organization of American Historians, Society of American Archivists Committee on Historians and Archivists, 1977.

Handlin, Oscar. *Truth in History.* Cambridge, Mass.: Harvard University Press, Belknap Press, 1979.

Hayward, Robert J. "Federal Access and Privacy Legislation and the Public Archives of Canada." *Archivaria* 18 (Summer 1984): 47-57.
Hedstrom, Margaret L. "Computers, Privacy, and Research Access to Confidential Information." *Midwestern Archivist* 6 (1981): 5-18.
Hixson, Richard F. *Privacy in a Public Society.* New York: Oxford University Press, 1987.
Hoff-Wilson, Joan. "Access to Restricted Collections: The Responsibility of Professional Historical Organizations." *American Archivist* 46 (Fall 1983): 441-47.
Holbert, Sue E. *Archives and Manuscripts: Reference and Access.* Chicago: Society of American Archivists, 1977.
Horn, David E. "The Development of Ethics in Archival Practice." *American Archivist* 52 (Winter 1989): 64-71.
International Council on Archives. *Archivum: Revue Internationale des Archives,* vol. 16. L'Ouverture des Archives a la Recherche: Actes du Congrès international extraordinaire des Archives, Washington, 9-13 mai 1966. Paris: Presses Universitaires de France, 1969.
____. *Archivum: International Review on Archives,* vol. 26. Proceedings of the 8th International Congress on Archives Washington, 27 September - 1 October 1976. Munich: K. G. Saur, 1979.
____. *Archivum: International Review on Archives,* vol. 29. Proceedings of the 9th International Congress on Archives London, 15-19 September 1980. Munich: K. G. Saur, 1982.
Jenkinson, Sir Hilary. *A Manual of Archive Administration.* Oxford: Clarendon Press, 1922.
Jourard, Sidney. "Some Psychological Aspects of Privacy." *Law and Contemporary Problems* 31 (Spring 1966): 307-18.
Kammen, Michael, ed. *The Past Before Us: Contemporary Historical Writing in the United States.* Ithaca, N.Y.: Cornell University Press, 1980.
Kitts-King, Jessie. "Privacy Act Implementation." *Records Management Quarterly* 13 (January 1979): 28-37.
Klassen, David. "The Provenance of Social Work Case Records: Implications for Archival Appraisal and Access." *Provenance* 1 (Spring 1983): 5-30.

Korman, A. T. "The Privacy Exemption to the Freedom of Information Act." *Journal of Legal Studies* 9 (1980): 727-70.

Ladenson, Alex. "Legal Problems in Administering Confidential Case Records." *SAA Newsletter* (May 1978): 10-11.

La Sala, James M. "The Impact of Privacy Legislation on Records Management." *Records Management Quarterly* 11 (January 1977): 10-12, 26.

Laudon, Kenneth C. *Dossier Society: Value Choices in the Design of National Information Systems.* New York: Columbia University Press, 1986.

Linowes, David. F. *Privacy in America: Is Your Private Life in the Public Eye?* Urbana, Ill.: University of Illinois Press, 1989.

Linowes, David F., and Michele M. Hoyman. "Data Confidentiality, Social Research and the Government." *Library Trends* 30 (Winter 1982): 489-503.

Linowes, David F., and Colin Bennett, "Privacy: Its Role in Federal Government Information Policy." *Library Trends* 35 (Summer 1986): 19-42.

Long, Edward V. *The Intruders: The Invasion of Privacy by Government and Industry.* New York: Frederick A. Praeger, 1967.

Lundvik, Ulf. "The Public's Access to Official Documents in Sweden: The Rules and their Consequences." *Government Publications Review* 10 (January-February 1983): 3-9.

Mayer, Dale C. "The New Social History: Implications for Archivists." *American Archivist* 48 (Fall 1985): 388-400.

McCloskey, H. J. "Privacy and the Right to Privacy." *Philosophy* 55 (1980): 17-38.

McDonald, Frances M. "Technology, Privacy, and Electronic Freedom of Speech." *Library Trends* 35 (Summer 1986): 83-104.

Medical Research Council of Canada. Working Group on Human Experimentation. *Ethical Considerations in Research Involving Human Subjects.* Ottawa: Medical Research Council, 1978.

Meisel, John. "Newspeak and the Information Society." *Archivaria* 19 (Winter 1984-85): 173-84.

Michael, James. "Official Information Law in the United

Kingdom." *Government Publications Review* 10 (January-February 1983): 61-70.

Miller, Arthur. *The Assault on Privacy: Computers, Data Banks, and Dossiers.* Ann Arbor, Mich.: University of Michigan Press, 1971.

Missen, Alan. "The Australian Freedom of Information Act." *Government Publications Review* 10 (January-February 1983): 43-49.

Mitchel, S. "Classified Information and Historical Research." *Government Publications Review* 10 (October 1983): 27-40.

Moore, Barrington Jr. *Privacy: Studies in Social and Cultural History.* Armonk, N.Y.: M. E. Sharpe, 1984.

Moseley, Eva S. "Sources for the 'New Women's History'." *American Archivist* 43 (Spring 1980): 180-90

Naugler, Harold A. *The Archival Appraisal of Machine-Readable Records: A RAMP Study with Guidelines.* Paris: Unesco, 1984.

Negley, G. "Philosophical Views on the Value of Privacy." *Law and Contemporary Problems* 31 (Spring 1966): 319-25.

Nejelski, Paul, ed.. *Social Research in Conflict with Law and Ethics* (Cambridge, Mass.: Ballinger Publishing Company, 1976).

Norton, Margaret Cross. *Norton on Archives,* ed. Thornton Mitchell. Carbondale, Ill.: Southern Illinois University Press, 1975.

Ontario Commission on Freedom of Information and Individual Privacy. *Public Government for Private People.* 3 vols. Toronto: Ministry of Government Services, 1980.

Ontario Provincial Secretariat for Resources Development. *Conference on Privacy, Initiatives for 1984.* Toronto: Provincial Secretariat for Resources Development, 1984.

Organization for Economic Cooperation and Development. Council of Ministers. *Guidelines Governing the Protection of Privacy and Transborder Flows of Personal Data.* Paris: Organization for Economic Cooperation and Development, 1981.

Parker, Richard. "A Definition of Privacy." *Rutgers Law Review* 27 (1974): 275-96.

Parr, G. J. "Case Records as Sources for Social History." *Archivaria* 4 (Summer 1977): 122-36.
Pennock, J. R., and J. W. Chapman, eds. *Nomos XIII: Privacy.* New York: Atherton Press, 1971.
Peterson, Gary M., and Trudy Huskamp Peterson. *Archives and Manuscripts: Law.* SAA Basic Manual Series. Chicago: Society of American Archivists, 1985.
Peterson, Trudy Huskamp. "After 5 Years: An Assessment of the Amended U.S. Freedom of Information Act." *American Archivist* 43 (Spring 1980): 161-68.
———. "Archival Principles and Records of the New Technology," *American Archivist* 47 (Fall 1984): 383-93.
Posner, Ernst. "Some Aspects of Archival Development since the French Revolution." *Archives and the Public Interest: Selected Essays,* ed. Ken Munden. Washington, D. C.: Public Affairs Press, 1967. 23-35.
Prosser, William L. "Privacy [a legal analysis]." *California Law Review* 48 (1960): 383-423.
Public Archives of Canada. *Guidelines for the Disclosure of Personal Information for Historical Research at the Public Archives of Canada.* Ottawa: Public Archives of Canada, 1984.
Rachels, James. "Why Privacy is Important." *Philosophy and Public Affairs* 4 (Summer 1975): 323-33.
Raines, John Curtis. *Attack on Privacy.* Valley Forge, Penna.: Judson Press, 1974.
Rankin, T. Murray. "The New Canadian Access to Information Act and Privacy Act: A Critical Annotation." *Government Publications Review* 10 (1983): 285-311.
Reiman, Jeffrey. "Privacy, Intimacy, and Personhood." *Philosophy and Public Affairs* 26(6) (1977): 31-36.
Reitman, Alan. "Freedom of Information and Privacy: The Civil Libertarian's Dilemma." *American Archivist* 38 (October 1975): 501-08.
Relyea, Harold. "The Rise and Pause of the U.S. Freedom of Information Act." *Government Publications Review* 10 (January-February 1983): 19-33.
Reynolds, Paul Davidson. *Ethical Dilemmas and Social Science Research.* San Francisco: Jossey Bass, 1979.
Robbin, Alice. "Ethical Standards and Data Archives." In

Secondary Analysis: New Directions for Program Evaluation, ed. Robert F. Boruch. San Francisco: Jossey Bass, 1978.

———. "State Archives and Issues of Personal Privacy: Policies and Practices." *American Archivist* 49 (Spring 1986): 163-75.

———. "Understanding the Machine-Readable Numeric Record: Archival Challenges, With Some Comments on Appraisal Guidelines." *Midwestern Archivist* 4 (1979): 5-23.

Robbin, Alice, and Linda Jozefacki, comps. *Public Policy on Health and Welfare Information: Compendium of State Legislation on Privacy and Access.* Madison, Wisc.: University of Wisconsin, Data and Program Library Service, 1983.

Rockefeller Archive Center. *The Scholar's Right to Know versus the Individual's Right to Privacy: Proceedings of the first Rockefeller Archive Center Conference.* December 5, 1975. n.p.: Rockefeller Archive Center, 1976.

Rosenfield, Frank A., "The Freedom of Information Act's Privacy Exemption and the Privacy Act of 1974." *Harvard Civil Rights-Civil Liberties Law Review* 11 (1976): 596-631.

Rule, James, et al. *The Politics of Privacy: Planning for Personal Data as Powerful Technologies.* New York: New American Library, 1980.

Russell, E. W. "Archival Ethics." *Archives and Manuscripts* 6(6) (February 1976): 226-34.

Schoeman, Ferdinand, ed. *Philosophical Dimensions of Privacy.* Cambridge, Mass.: Cambridge University Press, 1984.

Shank, Russell, "Privacy: History, Legal, Social, and Ethical Aspects." *Library Trends* 35 (Summer 1986): 7-18.

Shattuck, John. *Rights of Privacy.* Skokie, Ill.: National Textbook Co., 1979.

Shils, Edward. "Privacy: Its Constitution and Vicissitudes." *Law and Contemporary Problems* 31 (Spring 1966): 281-306.

———. "Social Inquiry and the Autonomy of the Individual." In *Social Research Ethics,* ed. Martin Bulmer. New York: Homes and Meier, 1982.

Sieghart, Paul. *Privacy and Computers.* London: Latimer New Dimensions, 1976.
Simmons, Ruth. "The Public's Right to Know and the Individual's Right to be Private." *Provenance* 1 (Spring 1983): 1-4.
Smart, John. "The Professional Archivist's Responsibility as an Advocate of Public Research." *Archivaria* 16 (Summer 1983): 139-49.
Smith, Robert Ellis. *Privacy.* New York: Doubleday, 1979.
____. *Compilation of State and Federal Privacy Laws.* Washington, D. C.: Privacy Journal, 1988.
Society of American Archivists, "Standards for Access to Research Materials in Archival and Manuscript Repositories." *American Archivist* 37 (January 1974): 153-54.
Stewart, Virginia. "Problems of Confidentiality in the Administration of Personal Case Records." *American Archivist* 37 (July 1974): 387-98.
Stoianovich, Troian. *French Historical Method: The Annales Paradigm.* Ithaca, N.Y.: Cornell University Press, 1976.
Tener, Jean. "Accessibility and Archives." *Archivaria* 6 (Summer 1978): 16-31.
Thomson, Judith Jarvis. "The Right to Privacy." *Philosophy and Public Affairs* 4 (Summer 1975): 294-314.
Turn, Rein. "Privacy Protection." *Annual Review of Information Science and Technology* 20 (1985): 27-50.
United States Congress. *Source Book on Privacy, Joint Committee Print of Senate and House Committees on Government Operations.* 94th Cong., 2nd Sess., Sept. 1976. Washington: U. S. Government Printing Office, 1976.
____. Office of Technology Assessment. *Federal Government Information Technology: Management, Security, and Congressional Oversight.* Washington, D. C.: U. S. Government Printing Office, 1986.
____. Department of Justice. Bureau of Justice Statistics. *Law Enforcement Assistance Administration: Confidentiality of Research and Statistical Data.* Washington, D. C.: Bureau of Justice Statistics, 1978.
____. ____. ____. *Privacy and Juvenile Justice Records.* Washington, D. C.: Bureau of Justice Statistics, 1982.

_____. _____. _____. *Criminal Justice Information Policy: Research Access to Criminal Justice Data.* Washington, D. C.: Bureau of Justice Statistics, 1983.

_____. _____. _____. *Juvenile Records and Recordkeeping Systems.* Washington, D. C.: Bureau of Justice Statistics, 1988.

_____. House of Representatives. *Oversight of the Privacy Act of 1974.* Hearings before a Subcommittee of the Government Operations, 98th Cong., 1st Sess., 7-8 June 1983. Washington, D. C.: U. S. Government Printing Office, 1983

_____. Privacy Protection Study Commission. *The Report of the Privacy Protection Study Commission*, 6 vols. Washington, D.C.: U. S. Government Printing Office, 1977.

_____. Senate. Committee on the Judiciary. Subcommittee on Administrative Practice and Procedure. *Freedom of Information Act Source Book: Legislative Materials, Cases, Articles.* Washington: U. S. Government Printing Office, 1974.

_____. Senate. Subcommittee on Oversight of Government Management of the Committee on Governmental Affairs. *Oversight of Computer Matching to Detect Fraud and Mismanagement in Government Programs.* Hearings before the Subcommittee on Oversight of Government Management of the Committee on Governmental Affairs. 97th Cong., 2nd Sess., 15-16 Dec. 1982. Washington: U. S. Government Printing Office, 1983.

Wagner, A. "The Policy of Access to Archives: From Restriction to Liberalization." *Unesco Bulletin for Libraries* 24 (March-April 1970): 73-76, 116.

Warner, Malcolm, and Michael Stone. *The Data Bank Society: Organizations, Computers and Social Freedom.* London: George Allen and Unwin, 1970.

Wasserstrom, Richard. "Privacy: Some Arguments and Assumptions." In *Philosophical Law: Authority, Equality, Adjudication, Privacy,* ed. Richard Bronough. Westport, Conn.: Greenwood Press, 1978.

Westfall, Gloria D. "Access to Official Information in Britain and France: A Study in Contrasts," *Collection Management* 6 (Spring/Summer, 1984): 159-76.

Westin, Alan F. *Privacy and Freedom.* New York: Atheneum, 1967.
Westin, Alan F., and Michael A. Baker. *Databanks in a Free Society: Computers, Record-Keeping and Privacy.* New York: Quadrangle Books, 1972.
Young, John B. *Privacy.* New York: Wiley, 1978.
Yoxall, Helen. "Privacy and Personal Papers." *Archives and Manuscripts* 12 (May 1984): 38-44.
Zimmerman, Diane L. "Requiem for a Heavyweight: A Farewell to Warren and Brandeis's Privacy Tort," *Cornell Law Review* 68 (1983): 294-367.
Zinn, Howard. "Secrecy, Archives, and the Public Interest." *Boston University Journal* 19 (Fall 1971): 37-44.

Index

Access to Information Act (Canada), 62, 131
  balancing of public and private interests in, 72-82
  Freedom of Information Act (U. S.) and, 74-76, 77, 78, 80, 82
  relationship to Privacy Act, 72-73
Ackerly v. Ley, 70
Anderson, R. Joseph, 110, 132
Annales school, 104-05
Anonymization procedures, 134-36, 137, 194
Archival administration of access
  difficulties associated with, 5-6, 92-93, 112, 114, 117-18, 127, 129-33
  ethical standards for, 197
  existing policies and procedures, 127-29
  ways of improving, 181-83, 191-94
  See also: Anonymization procedures; Archivists, education of, in privacy issues; Archivists, participation of, in privacy debates; Closed periods; Contracted access; Ethical review of research, archival procedures for; National Archives and Records Administration; National Archives of Canada; Screening procedures.
Archivists
  as public trustees, 5, 174, 194
  balancing of privacy and research interests, 114, 127-29, 148-49
  education of, in privacy issues, 195-98
  institutionalized altruism of, 198-99
  participation of, in privacy debates, 198-201
  professional obligations of, 5-6, 114, 174, 175, 180-81, 183
Arieff v. Department of the Navy, 65, 66, 67
Association of Canadian Archivists, 148

Bathory, Peter, 83
Baumann, Roland, 133, 138, 139, 192-93

Bay, Christian, 160
Beauchamp, Tom, 163
Bennett, Colin, 51, 52, 53
Bentham, Jeremy, 39-40
Bloch, Marc, 104-05
Bloustein, Edward, 16
Bogue, Allan, 136, 147
Bok, Sissela, 159, 170
Booms, Hans, 199
Bower, Robert, 162
Brandeis, Louis, 1, 16, 23-25
Brown, Robert Craig, 158
Burnham, David, 43

Capron, Alexander, 167
Case files, social welfare, 108-11, 112-14, 116, 132-33, 138-39, 174
Closed periods, 115, 183-84, 198
Cochran v. United States, 68
Committee on Privacy (Great Britain), 9-10
Computer matching
  for administrative purposes, 42-44, 52-54
  for research and statistical purposes, 88-89, 90-91, 134-35, 137
  See also: Socio-historical research, use of quantitative methods for demographic analysis.
Confidentiality
  confidential relationships and, 84-85, 169-70, 187-88
  legitimacy of expectation of, 71, 74, 171, 187-88
  principle of promise-keeping and, 169, 171
  statutory provision for, 70, 75, 128, 129-31

violation of, in research, 157, 163, 165-66, 169, 171
  See also: Anonymization procedures.
Consent
  implied, 168-69
  informed, 167-68
Contracted access
  existing procedures, 138-42
  problems with, 142-46
Cox, Richard, 198, 200

Dahlin, Michel, 107
Data linkage. *See* Computer matching.
de Gasparis, Priscilla, 162
Department of the Air Force v. Rose, 64, 65, 66, 67
Dollar, Charles, 136
Duchein, Michel, 46, 117, 144
Durkheim, Emile, 156-57
Dworkin, Ronald, 83-84, 173-74

Eckhart, Meister, 21
Ellsberg, Daniel, 26
Ellul, Jacques, 43
Ethical review of research archival procedures for, 184-92
Exemption Six (FOIA), 63-65, 68-72, 74, 82

Febvre, Lucien, 104-05
Ferri v. Bell, 67
Foucault, Michel, 38-40
Freedom of information, 4, 53-54, 61-62, 147
  See also: Access to Information Act (Canada); Freedom of Information

Index *221*

Freedom of information (continued)
    Act (U. S.); Freedom of Information and Protection of Privacy Act (Ontario); Right to privacy.
Freedom of Information Act (U. S.), 62, 63, 66, 68-77 *passim*, 80-88 *passim*, 118, 131, 139
    balancing of public and private interests in, 62-72
    relationship to Privacy Act, 62-63
Freedom of Information and Protection of Privacy Act (Ontario)
    balancing of public and private interests in, 85-88
Freedom of Information Law (France), 184
Freedom of inquiry, 147-48, 158-61
Fried, Charles, 12, 16
Functional separation, 191-92, 197

Gavison, Ruth, 13, 16, 17, 18, 19, 20, 26-27, 175
Getman v. NLRB, 68-69, 70, 77
Gillis, Peter, 113
Goffman, Erving, 17
Gough, J. W., 45
Grace, John, 44, 53
Greentree v. U. S. Customs Service, 63
Griswold v. Connecticut, 22
Grob, Gerald, 175

Hare, Richard, 170

Hedstrom, Margaret, 92, 129, 131, 134-35
Historical studies of demography, 106-11

Information Commissioner v. Minister of Employment and Immigration, 81
International Council on Archives, 115, 117, 118, 148

Janson, Carl-Gunnar, 156
Jenkinson, Sir Hilary, 174

Kelman, Herbert, 161, 164-66
Klassen, David, 115
Kuhn, Thomas, 157-58, 162
Kurzon v. Department of Health and Human Services, 70

Laberge, Danielle, 193
LaRose, Andre, 106
Law Reform Commission (Australia), 28
Linowes, David, 51, 52, 53
Lytle, Richard, 199

McCloskey, H. J., 11
MacIntyre, Alasdair, 161, 166
McWilliams, Wilson, 83
Mary Bland v. National Capital Commission, 78
Maxwell, Kimera, 71-72
Metropolit, 155-56
Miller, Arthur, 12, 26, 72, 83, 168-69
Miller, Frederic, 111

National Archives and Records Administration (U.S.), 116

National Archives and Records Administration (continued)
  administration of access to personal information for research and statistical purposes, 138, 139-41, 147
National Archives of Canada
  administration of access to personal information for research and statistical purposes, 79-80, 139, 141-42, 146-47
National Association of Atomic Veterans v. Dir., Defense Nuclear Agency, 68
National Capital Commission (NCC), 78-79
Naugler, Harold, 136
Nesmith, Tom, 105
Norton, Margaret Cross, 173
Nuremberg Code, 167
Nuremberg trials, 159

Ontario Commission of Freedom of Information and Individual Privacy, 84-85

Parker, Richard, 12
Parr, G. J., 109-10
Pentagon Papers, 146
Peterson, Gary, 131
Peterson, Trudy Huskamp, 131
Philadelphia Social History Project, 107
Pinkard, Terry, 172-3
Posner, Richard, 18
Prasad, S. N., 174
Privacy
  computer data banks and, 2-3, 27, 36, 40-42
  definitions of, 1-2, 9-14
  invasion of, in research, 156-57, 161-62, 165-67, 169, 171-72
  of information, 2, 3, 11-13, 14, 23, 25-28, 35-36, 41-42, 45
  public and private spheres, 36-37
  public interest and, 4-5, 62, 67-70, 72, 74-75, 76-80, 86-87, 92, 147
  social contract and, 45, 171
  See also: Confidentiality; Right to privacy
Privacy Act (Canada), 46-53 72-73, 79, 141
  balancing of public and private interests in, 72-81
  See also: Access to Information Act (Canada).
Privacy Act (U. S.), 46-53 *passim*
  relationship to Freedom of Information Act (U. S.), 62-63
Privacy Protection Study Commission (U. S.), 48, 49, 92, 130, 185, 191
Programme de Recherche en Démographie Historique, 106
Prossner, William, 15-16, 24

Rachels, James, 16
Rankin, Murray, 73
Reiff, Janice, 107
Reinsch, Roger, 71-72
Research and statistical uses of personal information, 79, 89-93, 136-37

Index 223

Research and statistical uses of personal information (continued)
existing law and practice regarding, 90-92, 128, 145-46
See also: Computer matching; Functional separation; Socio-historical research; Socio-historical research, moral evaluation of.
Right to know
See Freedom of information.
Right to privacy
as a right of living persons, 117-18
Common law protection of, 1, 22-27
Constitutional protection of, 22-23, 27
freedom of information and, 4-5, 53-54, 62-93
legislative protection of information privacy, 46-53
moral defense of, 1, 13-22
See also: Privacy; Privacy Act (Canada); Privacy Act (U. S.).
Robbin, Alice, 128-29, 148, 196, 197
Robertson, John, 158
Robles v. Environmental Protection Agency, 70
Roper, Michael, 103-04
Rosenberg, Carroll Smith, 108
Rowe, Judith, 127
Rule, James, 35-36, 44

Schafer, Arthur, 2, 20, 21, 41
Screening procedures, 138-39
problems with, 143-44

Shils, Edward, 4, 12
Sidis, William James, 17
Simmons, Ruth, 176, 181
Smith, Daniel Scott, 107
Société de Recherche sur les Populations, 106-07
Society of American Archivists
code of ethics, 116, 117, 175
definition of archivist, 174
Standards for Access to Research Materials, 115-16
Task Force on Goals and Priorities, 195-98
Socio-historical research
Annales school, the, 104-05
quantitative methods, use of for demographic analysis, 106-09, 112
See also: Case files, social welfare; Socio-historical research, moral evaluation of.
Socio-historical research, moral evaluation of
rights-based analysis, 164-73
risk-benefit analysis, 161-64
See also: Freedom of inquiry.
Stern v. FBI, 66
Stewart, Virginia, 113, 138, 139, 174
Swedish Data Inspection Board, 156

Tener, Jean, 112, 143
Thomson, Judith Jarvis, 14, 15

Warren, Samuel, 1, 16, 23-25
Warwick, Donald, 163-64
Washington Post Co., v. Department of State, 64
Wasserstrom, Richard, 18
Weizenbaum, Joseph, 40
Westin, Alan, 12

Williams, Raymond, 1-2
Wine Hobby, USA, Inc. v. IRS, 65, 68

Younger Committee
  See Committee on Privacy (Great Britain).

92009621

```
CD
986.5    MacNeil, Heather
.M33
1992       Without consent
```

DUE DATE